N Y N   R I F F A T

Award Winning Women's Empowerment Speaker

#HerRhythm

You Are More Than Your Survival Story

#HerRhythm by NYN RIFFAT

www.nynsdreams.com
Facebook.com/Nynsdreams

ISBN: 978-0-578-53463-3

Published by: Nyn's Dreams

Dedication

This book is lovingly dedicated to my beloved father Muhammad Rafiuddin Riffat.

My father passed away unexpectedly when I was in college. Just an hour before he breathed his last, we were talking and laughing. He died of a massive heart attack and passed away at the prime of his life while enjoying a successful career as a textile engineer. It shocked and devastated us all.

One does not realize the intensity of the pain of losing a loved one. It is when you wake up the next morning and see the sun rising, you realize that this sunrise and many more to come will still leave your soul dark and your home dull. It is when you sit for your dinner and you realize that the empty chair will never help you heal the loss. The pain gets deeper and deeper until it becomes part of your existence.

Even though it's been nearly twenty-three years since he died, there will never be a moment in my life when he will not be alive within me.

There are memories that time does not erase... Forever does not make loss forgettable, only bearable.

It was the year 1996 when I lost my father, the man who believed in my strength. I wish I could turn back time to be his little girl, but I know it can never happen to me again. I still remember tears rolling down my cheeks while I sat looking at my father lying breathless and helpless as death had embraced him forever.

But still, no matter how much time passes, no matter what takes place in the interim, there are some things we can never assign to oblivion, memories we can never rub away. They remain with us forever, like a touchstone.

Perhaps, I have yet not accepted the death of my father and so make sincere efforts to keep him alive. I can see him smiling when I live through his noble lessons of life... I can see his teary eyes when life treats me hard and hear him demanding me to be strong and be his happy little girl always.

My dad's teachings have helped me to come out of my pains and losses a little stronger and a little better. This book is a small yet authentic gesture to make him sparkle with pride in heavens beyond skies.

My father was the first man I ever loved. He comforted me, played with me, supported me and let me grow. His patience, quiet notion of complete understanding and unwavering love made me the woman I am today. He believed in me first. He danced with me first. He gave me all I could have ever needed, because he gave me love. And by giving me love, he taught me what love is and also what it isn't. He inculcated in me the belief that I could do anything.

I still remember how he stood behind me, while I struggled to gain my balance while learning how to ride the bicycle. How he insisted on removing those training wheels because he felt I was big enough to ride solo.

Even when the chips were down and I was at my lowest, he offered me such sound advice. As I sat next to my father with my first heartbreak, he comforted me and said, "Pick yourself up, this is just a phase and it too shall pass and one day you would know things better than you do now." He made me feel better and said the words I needed to hear.

I'm never really letting go of my father because I know that through any challenge I encounter or dream I decide to chase, he is still back there watching me, and waiting for me to win. I know that in my heart there is no love like the love of my father, and that part of me will always belong to my dad.

No matter where I am or how old I get, I will always love him. Till the seas go dry and rocks melt under the sun, he will be remembered, and I will always love him.

Acknowledgements

To all the people who were so kind and thoughtful during my toughest times. You lifted my spirits and helped me get through the long, lonely, painful days and nights. Thank you all.

Rashid - How did I get so lucky to have found you? for being there when I had lost myself, for believing in me and knowing what to say when it counted, for walking through hell with me. You have made my whole world brighter. I could write reams about it, but I'll just say it this way: I love you and thank you, soulmate.

Adam, my brother - could there ever be a better brother? Brother, confidant, guide, therapist, you name it, that's what you have been to me all my life. You were there through some of my darkest hours. Could I have made it without you? I don't know and I'm glad I did'nt have to find out. All my love and gratitude to you, my kid-brother.

My Extended Family (Satish, Shalini & Ritu)- Satish, how many times you have come to my rescue? You are a rare and special man. Ritu, my sister, my friend for life- I swear we were separated at birth, I love you so much. Shalini, thanks for being my daughter. You were my guardian angel when everything was falling apart and yes for letting **Raman** and my darling **Aadi** shower their unconditional love on me and my boys. I don't know what I would have done without you all. You all were balm on an aching soul. Love you all till eternity.

Rahat, Lauren & Areej- I will always be grateful for making my world a little brighter with your vibrant smiles, genuine care and affection. Thank you, my darlings.

Michael West, Anne Podesta & Cheney Butler- I'm sure that God had sent you here on this planet only to let the world feel and see the truth about angels. Thank you for always being my real cheer leaders. You were my real pros who knew how to give heart and soul.

Jessica Rector, my mentor - I've been blessed to have had the privilege of your advice and friendship over the years. It was you who pulled me out of the shame of a single mom fighting for her sons. Your guidance was a source of pride and inspiration to me. I wish you only the best; you deserve nothing less.

My Avery Dennison Family- I've loved working with you, we've had some good times. I can't count all the times you all have stood for me nor

I can repay you. Just know my gratitude is endless.

Jill Pergande, Kim Schnieder & Deena Baker - thank you for your wisdom, support and friendship. You taught me that miracles can happen if one woman stands for another. Bless you.

To my friends on the West Haven Chamber of Commerce & WOW - it's been a privilege to know you and to work with you. Thank you all.

Raza Noor, Lantz Preg, Michele Swinick & Kim Thompson-Pinder - I couldn't have made a better choice. What you all do is magic. Knowing you, working with you has enriched me in many ways I couldn't have imagined. I want to thank you all for your hard work, support and unflagging belief in my work.

Loving Paws - Dalenjer, Dane & Oscar - my four-legged babies always made me feel special. Your selfless love and hearty cuddles kept my belief alive that, *"Love makes the world go round."*

And towards the end, I have to thank the two people who believed in me, innocently abandoned all the luxuries of life, warmly turned my tears into smiles and gave me all the reasons to win and rise again and again.

Yes, my sons - Shaheer and Shayaal, your energy, optimism, love and support were unparalleled. I don't have enough superlatives in my vocabulary to express my appreciation and my love for what you did and for what you are. I will always be grateful to you for letting me nurture two exceptional human beings. I'm proud that someday I will leave this world with two men who have immense respect for women, who will always stand for the right and who will always know the power of truth and unconditional love.

Table of Contents

Introduction

The Best Doesn't Come Easy

*Today, wherever you are, whatever
regrets or circumstances you're dealing
with, take a moment to really appreciate
this gift we call life, and applaud.*

That day, standing in my driveway with my two sons and the few things we could carry with us, changed my life forever. At that moment, I didn't know how I would make it through the next minute, let alone the next hour or day. It was one of the hardest moments of life, but little did I realize that later I would be so thankful for it!

One of the hardest things about life is living through it. The life you dream of is wonderful and full of joy, but your reality is often very different. You look at what you are going through right now and you don't understand why it is happening. Can I share something with you?

The difficult things you conquer today are seeds that grow and change you for the life you dream about. That day for me was the beginning of a new stage of life that allowed me to write this book for you.

When there is a lot of struggle, chaos, problems, and opposition coming from everywhere, it is easy for you to want to go into a shell and not step out of it. The world starts speaking to you and you believe the lies it speaks. In time, that voice overpowers you and you forget what you are capable of accomplishing in this lifetime.

That happened to me. When I was young, I was my father's precious child even though I was a girl. He believed in me and encouraged me to become the 'best me' possible. My whole mindset growing up was yes, I can do it, I am capable and so I did well in my education.

On the other hand, when I got married it was a total shift because I was forced to believe that I am incompetent. I was regularly reminded that I am a diabetic, I am a woman who was not supposed to do or say things or put my voice on the table or have an opinion.

In my culture, the woman is supposed to be the perfect housewife that cooks, cleans and takes care of everyone else's needs besides her own – that's it. That was not me. I was always told that I am not a good wife.

When I got pregnant, it should have been a time of rejoicing. Instead, I was told that because I am diabetic, I shouldn't have a child because that child could come out with diabetes or other complications. In other words, a not-perfect child.

All of these things were hard on me and I started looking at myself as insufficient and not enough as a person. It started to impact my career and professional life as well. Even though I had the best ideas at work, I was afraid to speak up and share them. I would send it in writing or an email hoping that the manager or colleague would credit me with it, but it didn't happen.

Because I accepted the negative words spoken over me, I let the fear take over. I forgot everything I had been taught, including the strength that my father had crafted upon me, the real me. I forgot it because I started believing all that noise.

The message that I want to give to you is this: you must believe in yourself and the strength you have. People will be negative about you. They will find some reason to hate you, but you don't have to listen. You do not have to become the person they want you to be. My ex-husband and his family wanted me to change to their expectations of what they thought the perfect woman should be and for a time I listened and tried to change, but that was not who I truly was.

I am so thankful for the events that happened which freed me from those words, and I came back to the real me that had been hidden deep inside. The message I want to share with you is this: you are unique as a human being; you are a masterpiece. God created you for a reason, for a purpose, and nobody else should tell you what it is. You must listen to your inner voice. You connect with yourself first, before connecting with others.

The story of our life can be told in a thousand different ways. I realized that I am a divine project and so instead of telling my story over and over as a tragedy, I have chosen to call it an epic. I have gathered the boldness and courage to call it beautiful instead of calling it ugly.

Believe in yourself, I know when the time comes for me to leave this world, I can tell my sons that their mother was not perfect, but she had conviction. She fought with every ounce of her strength for what she thought was right. It's all we can ever do.

The Little Princess

Once upon a time, there lived a young princess surrounded by the magic of love and care. She once cried endlessly because her doll was stolen from her backyard. She thought her heart would never heal, but she was wrong.

She grew and soon found her solace in the adventures of being a teenager. Then she cried endlessly because her best friend was moving to a different place. She thought her heart would never heal, but she was wrong.

She grew and soon she found focus in her education and career. She then cried endlessly because she earned low grades. She thought her heart would never heal, but she was wrong.

Then the day came where her dreams of Prince Charming came true. She then cried endlessly because her prince walked over her and hated her. She thought her heart would never heal, but she was wrong.

She soon found her calling in raising her kids. She cried tears of happiness and sadness when her kids moved on in their lives, leaving her alone. She thought her heart would never heal, but she was wrong.

She soon found her conviction to celebrate her life. She realized that there were more days behind than ahead. Instead of crying she chooses to live each day with purpose knowing that all the tears she cried were not wasted. Those tears made her strong and now it was time to make the dreams of her heart a priority.

Life will hurt you, the world will tell you a thousand negative things, your name would be dragged in the mud a hundred times, but you have to celebrate the value that God has instilled in you. You are beautiful, you are sparkling. You are here to make a difference, so while overcoming life's challenges don't ever lose that very spark, that very light, that very grace which defines you.

Life will try to drag you down. Don't give in to anger, resentment, and jealousy. Remember that once a diamond was nothing special, but with enough pressure and time, it becomes spectacular, you are that diamond! Value, love, respect, and celebrate yourself as the masterpiece of the Creator.

The Confidence Factor

I love working with women and helping them to not only see their potential but live up to it. One of the biggest problems I see is the confidence factor, being small and not believing and trusting in themselves. It leaks into all areas of their lives including career whether at a job or their journey as an entrepreneur.

You make people doubt you when you doubt yourself. I want women to open up, step up. Don't be afraid to let people know how wonderful you are even at work. When was the last time you negotiated a salary instead of accepting what was offered?

As a manager, I see a marked difference in how men and women handle themselves during appraisals regardless of what region of the world they live, whether it's Asia, Europe, or the U.S.

I will ask them, "What do you want to achieve, what is it that you want to do, and where do you see yourself in five years?" Women are so reluctant to share because they often don't believe in their goals and in themselves.

When I appraise men, they know what they want and are not afraid to say it. They confidently share their aspirations to be at senior level or even in the board room. If I ask men, "Do you have any problems at work and how can I improve as a manager?" They tell me.

But if the same questions are asked to women, it is totally different and so painful. When I ask, "Where do you see yourself in five years?" They start listing the problems first. They don't see a future for themselves because they are conflicted over their roles as a woman. They are conditioned to believe that they should not and cannot have an advancing career because for a woman it is more significant to be defined as a responsible mother, a caring wife, and an obedient daughter.

I want to show you in this book that you can be exactly who you were created to be. You don't have to settle for second best. Throughout this book, I am going to be sharing with you my story. You will see how I started out strong and then how years of abuse had torn down my soul.

I will also share with you how I escaped from it, then had to fight Sharia law to get my sons. There were times I wondered if I would live through it. You don't fight that system as a woman and not fear for your life.

Then I will let you see how I made it to the US and how I have used my freedom to help others.

My story will encourage you to not give up. There is a bright future for you if you hold on and not let others determine your future. Learn from my story and start to dream again. It is time for your hopes and goals to come true. It is time for you to become the best 'you' possible.

Will you join me on this journey of self-discovery and faith? If I can make it through what I have, you can make it too.

In chapter 1, we look at the first important concept and that is 'believe in yourself'. Without that belief, I would still be trapped in the abuse of my past.

If you don't manifest what you want to be, if you don't believe in what you want to be. if you don't envision the version of you that you want to become, and if you allow people to tell you that you are not good enough or you can't do it, then you are being 'UNFAIR' to yourself.

Build the person you want to be. You have something unique and amazing to offer to this world. The purpose of your life is to figure out and calibrate your inner core to win your dreams. Don't let your lower self betray the gifts embedded in you.

Chapter 1:

Believe In Yourself

Our deepest fear is not that we are inadequate. Our deepest fear is that we are powerful beyond measure. It is our light, not our darkness, that most frightens us. We ask ourselves, "Who am I to be brilliant, gorgeous, talented, fabulous?" Actually, who are you not to be?

Marianne Williamson

There will be a time when your belief in yourself will be challenged and it is always at the times when you need it the most. The temptation to give up will be strong. Everything inside of you and outside of you is telling you that it is too hard, that it can't be done; that you are not good enough, strong enough or brave enough to face that challenge and win.

It is in those times of testing where your belief is proved and made even stronger. I went through many times where my conviction that "I can do this," was the only thing that got me through.

I want to especially encourage those who are entrepreneurs and leaders in any capacity. Your belief will be tested regularly. When you do something that is against what is considered normal, there will be opposition and you will be questioned whether you made the right decision or not, but it is those who continue to grow their belief in themselves who will succeed.

In this chapter, I want to share with you three stories from my life where I had to make a choice to believe in myself or fail. You will see my struggles and how I needed to find solutions to tough situations and how belief carried me through. Let what I went through give you the courage to conquer your own obstacles and build a stronger belief in yourself.

Soccer Balls

Very early in my career, I worked for a global exporting and sourcing business in Pakistan that had its head office in the US. My office was asked to source soccer balls for companies like

Nike and Adidas. The meeting was planned to take place in Hong Kong.

My boss came up to me and said, "I would like for you to go to Hong Kong and be the bridge between the manufacturers from Pakistan and the buyers from the U.S. and you will need to prepare the presentation."

I am amazing in apparel and footwear and I love marketing and connecting with people, it is one of the best parts of being a business strategist; but soccer balls, I know they are round and that is it. I'm also a person to whom numbers do not come naturally, I have to put a little extra effort to comprehend and have conversations around them.

When my boss told me that I have to create a number-driven presentation, I knew that I was in serious trouble. I tried to get out of it by telling my boss that I knew nothing about soccer balls, but he told me I was the one that was going.

I went home, and I was so scared about getting the numbers right, and what would happen if I got them wrong and the meeting attendees figured it out and the deal fell through because I couldn't get things right. I was so afraid that I didn't sleep for the whole night.

[13]

The next morning when I got to the office, I had a decision to make. I could stay indecisive and let fear control the situation or I could find a way to make it work for me. It was not an easy decision. Fear is powerful, but my father had instilled in me that I could do anything, so there had to be a way to get this presentation done.

I started working on the presentation in a very different way. I discussed child labor. I discussed where soccer balls are made around the world and why Pakistan is the best. I told them how thin fingers are needed to do the knotting correctly to make the ball high quality and women and children work in their homes doing this to support themselves.

I also talked about how the equation of manufacturer and importer would work together if this business materializes. That was how I did my presentation. Obviously, I put some numbers in the presentation, but I did it the way that felt best to me.

When I went to Hong Kong and delivered my presentation, everybody started writing to my boss that she's the best because she brought the community piece into it and how world-class brands could make a difference in less privileged countries.

Here is what I learned from that experience. It is about accepting my weaknesses, but then, choosing to believe in myself and do it in a way that I know will make an impact and influence others. Just because you are not good at something, shouldn't stop you from doing it. You bring all of those pieces together, your weaknesses, your strengths and work around them to make it happen.

My Marriage Was Over

I had never been a good wife or a good daughter-in-law to my ex-husband and his family. My health, career, and approach to life made me undesirable, so he went and found someone that was more submissive and would take care of him. There was only one problem. I was still living in the house, so he came up to me one day and told me that I had to leave NOW. He was done with me and I was to get out right away.

Then he went to our kids. My oldest son was 12 at that time and my younger one was four and didn't have any idea what was going on. He asked my oldest, "Do you want to go with your mom or stay here with me?" My son without a second thought said that he wanted to be with his Mom.

My ex-husband was not pleased and said, "If you go with your mom, you will be begging on the streets because she can't give you the life that I have given you." He said that because he was rich and felt that he held all the cards. My son said, "That it's okay, but I want to be with her." Those words of my son have been my inspiration and motivation ever since.

We had enough time to grab a few things. How do you know what to take? You don't, so we packed a few clothes, my son's school uniform and bag and that was it.

My youngest he went to his dad and asked, "Can I take my PlayStation?" The answer was "No," so he left his mountain of toys, and the three of us walked out of the house.

I had a driver, so we sat in my car and we just drove around for a couple of hours not knowing what to do. The driver finally asked, "What do you want me to do?" Up to the point I was in shock and had not thought it through. As I did, I thought of my family home and had him take us there.

The house had been closed up for a long time but at least it was a place to stay. I could have gone to my brother's and he might have taken me in

[16]

as part of his responsibility, but I didn't want to do that.

That night was hard. Everything reminded me of my dad and the good times that we had there together. His words were haunting me in my mind because he believed in me so much. That whole night I was crying and thinking, "What has happened?" I felt like I was a failure because I was trying to be in that marriage for my kids. I had tried everything, and it didn't work. Now that I am thrown out of the house and my kids believe in me, what am I supposed to do? Am I that strong that I will be able to handle everything alone?

Something happened at dawn. The night had been so dark both physically and, in my soul, but with the dawn, I realized that I can do this. I called my boss in India and said, "I've been thrown out of the house with my kids and I need a couple of days to figure everything out." He said, "Of course, if you need anything just let us know."

Although he extended his full support offering me a lawyer and a place to live, I refused because I knew that it's my struggle and I have to figure it out. I needed to learn how to live through this and build a better life for my sons and myself.

The Power of Belief

So, belief is one of the core basics of every life. If you don't believe in your values, if you don't believe in your own strengths, and that if you try, you will succeed, then all of the negative noise that is happening around you captures you, conquers you and then you don't do anything.

When you were born you had a strong belief that you are surrounded by people who are meant to protect you. You believed that your mother would take care of you. Then you believed that your father would be there and support you, then that your teacher would help guide you.

But what happens is as the time passes, as you grow, the negativity that comes from people around us starts taking a portion of your thoughts. When people are rude to you or their actions are not right it starts governing the belief system in you. Unknowingly, you start looking at yourself from the space of judgement and you start layering your existence with the concrete of disbelief, comparison, worry, and shame.

Then self-doubt and fear start to creep in and the more noise you hear the more you believe it. You stop believing in God or the presence of an infinite source of power upon you.

My belief in myself started to erode when I went to college and saw how the boys were treated better than me. I stopped standing up for myself when a boy would get an A+ and I only got an A, even though I deserved the full mark. I wasn't given certain projects that I wanted to do because I was a girl.

It only got worse when I got married. I was shunned by my husband's family because I was diabetic. When I got pregnant, all my ex-sister-in-law said was, "Oh, my God, Allah can even bless people who are not capable of conceiving."

Because I started accepting everything that was coming from society, and other people, it was directly challenging my personal belief and giving more food to self-doubt. That's the reason I stayed in that abusive marriage because my belief was shattered or disrupted, and I accepted all of the negative stuff about myself as normal.

The same is for you. When you start accepting the negativity, it becomes a hindrance for you to believe in yourself, and then to believe in something above you, such as God.

Remember, when you get rid of your self-doubt and fear, your absolute success will rise.

You Can't Be It If You Can't See It

I grew up with the thought that, "If you look at a tree long enough, it will move." We see what we want to see.

When my younger son was five and a half years old, he was chosen to act the role of a king in his pre-school drama evening. He was very happy because he got to start his rehearsals the very next day. After two days his teacher called me that I have to prepare his costume to be a rat and not a king. Upon getting into details, I was informed by the teacher that during the practice, my little one chose to switch to a rat. Like the teacher, I was also surprised as to what made him make this decision.

Later that night I asked the little one if he chose to play the role of a rat. To my surprise, he nodded in confirmation. His elder brother started laughing and called him silly. But the little one said in his innocent words, "Mama, I sat on the throne with a hard face, nothing to do. It was so boring. But the kids who were playing the role of rats were dancing and they made the king and his son smile too. I decided to join them."

[20]

His brother made fun of him that your friends will call and tease you as a rat, to which he replied, "No, I am a rat like Stuart Little."

Later he performed in the drama evening as the rat and did his performance so enthusiastically that the entire audience giggled, smiled and clapped. He won 'The Cutest Rat' award while the king was just a character in the play. He knew that he would be a 'celebrity rat' like Stuart Little and he was.

You are what you think you are. If you don't think you'll be successful, you won't. You can't be it, if you can't see it. Your life is limited to your vision. If you want to change your life, you must change the vision of your life.

Feed Your Belief

You only have so many tomorrows and none of us know how many they are. If you know that the next few days would be your last days in this life, would you be 100% happy? Would you be in absolute contentment? The answer that would come from the majority of us would be a "No."

How about you? You live an unfulfilled life because you refuse to believe in your dreams, in your uniqueness and spent your years to matching someone else's picture of perfection.

[21]

You surrendered your authentic self and lived a life that was far away from your purpose.

Belief is fueled by what you feed it. So, if you start focusing and continue to listen to what others are saying about you – your capabilities will starve.

You develop your belief when you start respecting your core values and your passion. When you start believing in yourself, you start putting yourself out in the world to tell them, this is my passion, these are my core values. How can I be of help to you so that you become that person whose dreams are aligned with the inner authentic voice?

Become your own best friend. When you are developing a friendship, you spend time with that person. You get to know what they like, and you give it to them. You see what is amazing in that person and confirm it. You need to do the same for yourself. Get to know and like yourself, as you would do to a best friend. That person is not perfect, but you accept them just the way they are and help them become a better version of their own being. Practice the same rule of friendship with yourself.

When you believe in yourself and God or a higher power above, nothing is impossible for you. You can reach your goals and your dreams. Now is the time to start. Will it be hard at first? Possibly, but as you step out in faith, it will become easier and easier.

In the next chapter, we will look at another important aspect of life and that is self-respect. Once you believe in yourself, this is the next level.

Every day that you wait puts your dreams at risk.

Chapter 2:

Respect Yourself

Get off the clearance rack and I mean RIGHT NOW! If you don't value and respect yourself wholeheartedly, no one else will either!

Respecting yourself is a subject that is near and dear to my heart. I have been on both sides of the fence. There were times that I did and then I gave up some of it for twelve years and now I finally have it all back!

Here is my definition of respect:

Respect means to have the mindset to accept that every living being on this earth is of some value and they are here for a purpose, for a reason. God created everyone, and they are valuable.

Including you! The most important respect to have is to respect and value yourself.

Why Women Don't Respect Themselves

Women are so good at doing this. They have mastered this since the world came into being. When you were born you had total self-respect. You were happy, learning and growing. Anytime you needed something you let the world know through your cries and mom and dad would meet it. You are your natural self and the world has not touched you yet.

But then you start learning from the world, you start believing others, and that is the time when you start disrespecting yourself. For example, you get told things like 'walk straight because that is the only way to walk'. Don't wear heels because your foot will cramp, or it is not acceptable in your culture. When you start listening to all of those noises around you, you start disrespecting yourself by not listening to what you want.

Because you start to listen to others, you start doubting yourself. You go into the store and you love heels, but you go look for flats because someone said you were too tall for heels. You want to be accepted by society and so you buy the flats that you would not even consider otherwise. You have disrespected yourself for the sake of someone else. You do it because you want to be accepted.

A woman's need for acceptance is strong. We were built to be social, interactive creatures who work together to get results. We do not work well when we are isolated. That is why we are willing to change who we are to appease others and camouflage the disrespect that we bring to ourselves with the sole purpose of "fitting in" with words like flexibility, adaptability, etc.

How I Lost My Self-Respect

When I was a little girl, my father taught me to respect myself. He taught me how to make decisions and then stand by them. When my decisions were different from the ones he wanted, I was still his blue-eyed girl and he would respect what I wanted or needed.

In my culture, if you were a smart girl you could become an engineer or doctor, but that wasn't where my heart lay. I wasn't interested in those things. I loved everything about apparel, fabrics, and the manufacturing of them. So, I took up the business and marketing of textiles as a career and I was happy.

But then things changed…

I was interning when I met my husband and we decided to get married. He came from a rich and conservative Islamic family and he loved how free I was. He told me he wanted me to be part of his family, so I could be a good influence on other women in his family, especially the young women who will get to see, meet and live with an educated woman and will aspire to be authentic and acknowledge their own worth.

He knew when he proposed that I was diabetic, that I worked for a living and that I wore clothes that were non-traditional for our culture. He went into the relationship knowing everything. I hid nothing from him. On the outside, he seemed so supportive of who I was.

It wasn't even 60 days into the marriage that I started to learn the truth.

I had dressed up in a sleeveless dress one evening to go out with my husband and family, and the moment I came out of my room, my mother-in-law and my husband looked at me and they said, "It's not appropriate. You are not decently dressed, it's inappropriate."

I immediately went back and changed, wore a full-sleeve dress and then I joined them for that evening. From that day up to the end of my marriage 12 years later, I made sure that I was not wearing anything which in their definition is revealing or inappropriate or indecent. Although, that wasn't me, because I loved wearing sleeveless dresses.

I did it because I wanted to be accepted in that culture – accepted by them.

The label I wore was, 'She changed herself for her husband.' This is what we do. Every woman is brutal to herself when she does this. When she changes.

I'm not saying that if your partner, or dad, or your brother likes you to wear the red dress, and to honor them you buy and wear a red dress, that's okay. That's once in a while. I am talking about the changes that we bring into our lives forever. When we change ourselves to please someone else.

To wear something occasionally because another person likes it on you is showing love. To change who you are and what you wear or do all the time only to be loved and accepted is wrong. It is disrespecting yourself.

It's the same in the workplace, whether it's your business, a corporation or a small company that you work for. When women are out there in the workplace, they start doing things that would

[29]

not make their managers or colleagues uncomfortable and get them accepted. They won't question things because they feel that if they do, they will not be accepted and will be judged.

Have you ever experienced that? If you have then you are disrespecting yourself. You are allowing someone in a position of authority to control you and change you. That should never happen in the workplace.

God did not create women to serve men. He created her as an equal partner, that is why she is taken from Adam's rib. To stand side by side with the man. If she was to be subservient to him, then why didn't he make her from his foot? God gave her everything he gave a man, a mind to think with, a heart to feel with and a body to do things with.

Another area where I gave in was with my career. He knew that I worked and would continue to work after we were married. He didn't need my money and never ever claimed his right on my earnings, yet he made it difficult for me in other ways.

After we were married, he started to ask me to give it up and become a respectable wife and daughter-in-law. It got worse when I was pregnant. Through it all, I refused to quit my job, but then he started putting conditions on my work. I couldn't be in a car with my fellow employees, I had to be home by a certain time, I couldn't go to office parties and my fellow employees were not allowed in my home. The biggest one was I was not allowed to travel.

All of these I accepted and obeyed because I was trying to be his good wife and still be me. It was hard. I did it because that is what a 'good wife does', but it was killing my soul in the process.

I was living two different lives. The moment I was in my office I was the real queen, working, talking to people, making things happen, keeping deadlines, working with the teams, encouraging them, but I would avoid projects that would require travel or extended working hours.

So, there were things that I was doing at work because of my husband, and unknowingly, they were hurting my career.

How To Respect Yourself

Simple. You have to believe in yourself. Everything begins with that. When you believe in yourself, you value yourself. I have a simple question for you – why do you respect others?

You respect others because you don't want to hurt their feelings. You respect others because you want to look good. You respect others because that's the normalcy of society. You respect others because you want to be valued as a fine human. These are the reasons why you respect others.

Why can't these reasons be the ones for you to respect yourself? Why can't you say, "No," when you don't want to do something? You can be kind and still say, "No." Why do you have to accept things which you believe are not the right things for you? Why can't you respect your own self?

The second way to build self-respect is to be sure about your values. What is important to you? For me, my strongest value is truth; lies make me go crazy. I lost my self-respect because I believed in my ex-husband's lies.

I was not true to my value of being truthful towards the truth. Whenever you compromise your values, you lose your self-respect. You have to believe in yourself, and you have to stand up for that. When you stand up for yourself, you create self-respect.

Self-respect is never rude. It does not say, "It's my way or the highway," that's not self-respect.

When somebody is trying to tell you something, there has to be logic in it and it must align with your values. If not, you respectfully must disagree. When you have self-respect, you can also show others respect, even when your opinions differ.

Never compromise on your values to please someone else. It is never worth it.

No matter how much you respect yourself, there's going to be times when people just don't respect you back. Let me share a story about a complete stranger who demonstrated to me the power of self-respect.

A few months after my divorce, I was at a government office to apply to change my marital status from married to divorced on my legal documents.

At the Information Desk, I was welcomed by a decent man who had the information I needed. He seemed hesitant to help me when he found out I was divorced but he did. Another lady in her late fifties came in and her words changed my life. She asked to change her marital status and last name back to her maiden one.

I immediately turned to listen as to how would he attend this lady. Here he questioned, "Is it because of death?" and the lady replied, " No, divorce after 33 years of marriage and now I'm 59". The man replied, "Do you still want to go through this hassle of a name change?" He obviously wasn't supportive of her decision.

The lady said, "Yes, I want to live and make my own identity. I gave my youth to this man and his children, now I want to see what I can give to myself. I disrespected myself long enough and even if it's just a day before my death, I want to honor this woman inside me. I need her to forgive me and I want her to know that she is respected for what she is and not by how the world has known her."

Her words demonstrated to me the power of self-respect and I have never forgotten them. When I feel tempted to change who I am, her words come back and remind me that even if it is only for one day, I will honor myself.

It is only when you respect yourself that you can move forward in life. In the next chapter, I share something very personal with you. I do it in the hopes that you won't be caught in the same way I was.

Chapter 3:

Don't Be in Denial

Denying the truth does not change the facts.

Unknown

I spent twelve years in denial about my marriage and I still can't believe I did that. The day he chose me to be his life partner, I assumed that I was the person he wanted for the rest of his life. But the opposite was true. I started changing myself, to get the acceptance of his family, and appearing as a faithful, loyal wife, sister-in-law, and daughter-in-law.

I was in denial that this man who claimed that he loved me for who I was is now saying that he hates me for all of those reasons. He and his family lied to me, but to be honest, those people were still far more truthful than what I was with myself.

When their true colors came out, they did not change. They were open in saying what they want, in fact, they were imposing it. They were yelling at the top of their lungs, this is what we want, while I was in denial telling myself that this is temporary, everything will change, it's not meant to hurt me, it's for my betterment and happier life.

The restrictions he placed on me like not travelling, no male friends and not being open-minded, were (in my opinion at the time) because he was thinking something good about me. I was in complete denial that whatever was happening to me was hurting me. That's the worst part.

Because of that denial, I accepted everything that was happening to me in a negative way, personality-wise, perspective-wise, and health-wise. I started to believe their lies that I was not good enough. These things were happening because it's my fault.

If I wanted to travel for work for two days, I am an irresponsible mom. The lies they told me became my truth.

When I hit the next stage of denial, I told myself, "Yes, I can see the blood figuratively dripping from my body, but it's not hurting, and I don't need a band-aid, I don't need anything." Even though someone else was mentally, emotionally and physically abusing me, I have to find out why the blood is there, and ultimately it is my fault. I'm bleeding, but I deserve to bleed.

When I started believing in all of what was said to me, the self-doubt and the fear became my disease. I started doubting myself. I feared everything. My thoughts were, "How can I leave this marriage? What will happen to my kids? What will society say? That this woman left her husband because she was not allowed to work, or he would ask her not to wear sleeveless, are these the reasons to leave a relationship? What will I do for money?" The self-doubt and fear would hold me back. The funny thing was these were lies. I was financially stable enough to support myself and my boys.

It is time for me to share this openly. I was mentally, physically and emotionally abused for twelve years. I don't remember romance and love. All I remember is nights when I cried endlessly.

[37]

I faced horrors during those years of my marriage. I don't know which tore my soul apart more the terror I felt the first time when I witnessed the violence, or the numbness that came after it started to become ordinary.

I was silly and naive and continued to hope day after day that things could someday get better when really, I was decaying and dying inside. During these years, I had felt the cold and darkness coming and I knew that this fairy tale would have a tragic end, but every time I wanted to free myself, I found myself being dragged back in.

I looked at my two adorable sons and thought I would someday be able to save my marriage for their well-being. Now I realize that my husband knew that he was walking over the three of us.

I can still see the dark circles around my eyes sinking deeper and deeper and my skin resembling a fresh corpse, because my soul had suffered, and it had started surfacing physically. I was trapped in self-denial and it is a place that I never want any woman to put herself. It is my hope that by reading this book, your eyes will be open, and you will see the truth.

Why Self-Truth Is Important?

Women, in general, have been taught that it is more important to change yourself to become what others want you to be than to be your best self.

That leads to women accepting lies as truth. It is time for women to learn that you can be yourself and be accepted and loved.

When I was married and wanted to buy something for my husband, there would be all these doubts, even if it was something I wanted him to have. I would question myself, "Will he like it? Will he accuse me of spending too much money on it? Will he tell me to take it back?" I couldn't buy something for him just because I wanted to.

My question to you is, "Why can't you be true to yourself?" If you are out, and you want to buy something for your spouse, why shouldn't you? That's what we do with our kids. When I am going to buy something for my 10-year-old, and I find something that he will like, I don't question myself, I just buy it. I wouldn't think, "Should I call him, should I ask him, or what price it is?"

The same directive goes for work. You should be able to be yourself and succeed. You are not perfect. There are things that you are great at and things that you are not. You should be able to express that and not try to change to please someone else.

Like we shared in a previous chapter, I'm not a numbers person. I am true to myself that I'm not a numbers person. So, if somebody is coming and saying something about or questioning my numbers; I encourage them to double check my work. It is my weak area and if they can fix it up, I am thankful, not offended.

On the other side, I am great at speaking and my team knows it. It is my strength and passion. I will be the first to volunteer and they will let me do it.

So, the truth is so important. The moment you start accepting things about you, the truths about you, whether they are weaknesses, or all of the positive things, you will have the self-respect, you will have confidence and you will never be in denial.

What happens within you determines what happens in your life.

The surest way to make more of your life is to become more aware of what's in you, and to expand your definition of what is possible. I've truly come to believe that if we can find the courage to stay true to ourselves and do the things that make us feel most alive, we do not only do ourselves a favor, but the world a favor too.

Can I share one other thing with you? When someone gives you a compliment, accept it. Stop justifying what is great about you and trying to give reasons for it. When you do that, it shows that you don't truly believe it. For example, you get a new haircut, and someone tells you how much they like it. Don't say, "Well, it only cost me $20." Say, "Thanks, I love it too."

Self-truth empowers you. It gives you the confidence to be who you truly are and love yourself for the good, the bad and the ugly because we all have that within us. Being truthful to yourself is acceptance of both your weaknesses and your strengths.

Sometimes the one thing you need is the one thing you are afraid to do. For instance, there are some who said I should have fought harder or longer than I did for my marriage, that I should have changed more to make him happy. But in the end, fighting for love that was already gone felt like trying to live in the ruins of a lost city. I had to step over the false belief that there will be a verse, quote, phrase or talk that will magically make me feel content and complete. It made me finally realize that I left without ever leaving.

This type of journey is the scariest road one will ever travel. However, it is the road God will never let you travel alone as God will Himself travel with you; but only if you are true to yourself and your core values.

In the next chapter, I will share with you something that even to this day, I don't understand why I did it.

Chapter 4:

Don't Stay In The Misery

You shall know the truth and it will set you free.

The Bible

One question that I have been asked is 'why did I stay for twelve years in an abusive relationship'? I wish I could give you a straight answer on that, but I can't.

But…

What I do want to do is explore that time-period. What happened, how I felt and what you can do to make sure that you never end up in a situation like that, or if you recognize yourself in my story that you will know what to do.

Like I shared in the previous chapter, my ex-husband went into the marriage with his eyes wide-open to who I was. I hid nothing. I was unique and different and confident in who I was.

My family, and especially my father, believed that education is the key to everything. Every family member must have a career, including women. Women are complete as human beings and deserving of respect and opportunities, just like men are. A woman should never be under the shadow of a man and depend completely on him for support.

After the abuse started, I asked myself many times during those years, "Why did I marry him?" The answer is simple. I believed his lies when he told me that he loved me the way that I was. I was brought up to believe in people, to trust a person until proven otherwise. He told me what I wanted to hear, and I accepted it as truth.

For a long time, I questioned why he would do this to me. I think I may have come up with an answer. He loved being in control and saw me as a challenge. I was everything his culture told him I shouldn't be. I was smart and independent. I spoke my mind. I knew what I wanted and was looking for a man who would partner with me in life, not control me. I didn't need a man to be complete but wanted someone who would love and encourage me to be the best woman I could.

I was a challenge he could not refuse. His goal was to break me and make me subservient to him, so he could prove to the world that women were beneath him. It is the only reason to explain his sudden 'change of heart' so quickly into the marriage. In as little as thirty days, I knew that I had made a mistake.

It is hard for me to share all these personal details with you. It brings up a lot of memories that I want to leave in the past, but I will do it because I want you to see what the control and abuse looked like. Maybe you will read this, and you won't see yourself in it. If that is you, be thankful. Maybe you are reading this so that you can understand and help someone else.

But maybe you are like me and in denial of what is going on. If you read this and recognize yourself in it, then take it as a warning that your life isn't the way it should be, and you need to do something about it.

What My Life Looked Like

Let's look at three areas: control, respect, and emotional abuse. My ex-husband wanted to control every area of my life, and he would have if I let him.

I put my foot down when it came to working. I was not giving up my career, so my husband took another path. He said I could work, but put all these terms and conditions on it, such as:

> ➢ Family events came first over work. I was constantly being forced to take time off work or reschedule important work meetings because I had to conform to his schedule.

> ➢ I could not travel with co-workers. If we had to travel to a meeting, I would have to go by myself.

> ➢ I was not allowed to make work trips outside of the local area. Even though I was the best person to go, I would have to refuse.

> ➢ I was not allowed to socialize with my co-workers after work and they were not allowed at my house.

> ➢ I was made to feel like an irresponsible mom and wife anytime work required a bit of extra time from me.

Every time I turned around, I was expected to make compromises. My ex-husband and his family had concerns about what I wore, what I didn't wear, what I should wear, what I shouldn't be wearing. When it started it came as a surprise and I wasn't prepared for it.

It's not that I would wear a bikini or revealing dresses around the city, but I wouldn't cover my head, or wear complete conservative clothing. They were demanding that I do that, but I put my foot down and said, "No, I have never covered my head since my birth, so why would you expect me to do that now?" Of course, that answer only brought on more anger and hatred towards me.

Respect

I grew up in a family where your privacy is respected. When I was younger, mobile phones were not common, so everybody would use landlines.

If somebody would call me from my college or school and that person happened to be a boy, the only question that my dad or anybody who answers the phone was, "Can you hold on for a second, or do you mind telling your name?" They wanted to know the name so that they could convey the message to me. Then they would tell me somebody's on the phone for me and that was it.

Same thing with the mail. No one at my house would even think about opening my mail and I would not touch theirs. We respected each other. This was normal and ethical for me. Each person deserved respect.

When I got married, I would never ever check my husband's phone, even if his phone was ringing. If he said to answer it, I would, otherwise I wouldn't even see who is calling. I never checked his texts either.

Even if his mail sat on the table for two or three days, I never touched it. It was marked to him and I respected that. I also never went through his wallet either. I had my own money and he had his.

Respect is incredibly important to me. My father taught me that respect is essential in life.

On the other side, he would check my phone when I came back from the office. If I was in the restroom, he would go through my calls and my messages and everything. If any letter would come and I wasn't there, anybody in the house would open my mail and see what it is.

I felt violated and offended and there was nothing I could do. I couldn't go to his family about this because they would accuse me of being a bad wife. When I would try to express my feelings to my husband, he would accuse me of trying to hide something and I would never hear the end of it. It got to the point where I wouldn't say anything because the consequences weren't worth it. The character assassination was brutal.

Emotional Abuse

Almost every day I was told what a bad wife, daughter-in-law and sister-in-law I was. My ex-husband and I both worked, and our jobs were important, so I didn't text my husband and disturb him at work unless it was important. Because I didn't need to be texting him all day, he would accuse me of not loving him, not caring about him. When I respected his privacy and didn't go through his things, he accused me that I was not a loving wife. The truth is had I gone through his mail, his texts or his phone, I would have gotten an even worse response.

Both pregnancies were incredibly hard emotionally. I was constantly being told that my babies would be deformed or sickly because I was diabetic. There was no rejoicing that I was going to have a child, just ridicule.

Everything I did from the smallest to the biggest things – I was questioned, I was challenged, I was discouraged, and this was not helping me at all.

It didn't matter what I did, it was never good enough. He wanted me mentally, emotionally and physically dependent on him for everything, and since I wasn't, I paid the price for it. I gave up a lot of myself in trying to please him and his family, but I would not give up the real me. That I held onto, I could not let that go.

Why did I stay? I was always seeing it as something that will improve, I was hoping it will improve, I was in denial that I was being hurt. I would justify it by saying to myself that my boys needed their father and that they would suffer emotionally and financially if I left.

Unhealthy Situations For Women

Personally, and professionally, the first and the foremost thing women try to do is fit in.

And that's the worst thing that they do. When you try to fit in, you are hiding or compromising yourself. Whether it's at a personal level or a professional level. I kept on trying to fit into a culture where I wasn't even accepted, and it happened even professionally.

There are times when women in their jobs, careers or businesses, where they do things to make sure that they fit in and that they are accepted. They don't want to be thought of as a failure.

Here is something I have observed: when a man fails it's because of lack of resources, lack of time and energy, or maybe his health, blah, blah, blah.

His failure would be blamed more on the circumstances.

When a woman fails, it's because she is a woman. She is too strong-minded or too loud because she is a woman, and you know women are emotional.

Women themselves will become the reason for their failure, rather than their circumstances. That failure could have happened to a man too, but a woman is labeled. I have seen this everywhere from Pakistan to North America.

It is very important for a woman to respect her own self and stop doubting her own existence. The best way to get out of these situations is not to get into these situations in the first place.

If you are in an abusive relationship, the first and the foremost thing is that you need to have a dialogue with your partner; about what you are not liking, that you are uncomfortable, and this is not right and unfair.

If he says, "Okay, I will improve, and we can work toward that," you give people that chance. But if somebody does it again, and is not making the right attempt, then it is time to start working on an exit plan. It's a signal that is being sent to you by God, by a higher power, by the universe, that it's not going to work. Because if people are lying to you and not making an effort to make you feel comfortable; that means that they don't want that relationship.

Don't stay in that state of denial and misery, as it will only worsen the situation for everybody around you. If you have kids, they are the ones who will suffer the most. If you don't have kids, everybody around you, whether it's your mom, your dad, your brothers, your sisters, your friends, everybody will suffer because you're staying in a state of denial and misery.

[52]

Choose To Get Out

I hope that this chapter has opened your eyes and allowed you to see that you have worth. I gave up my worth for twelve years and I will never do that again.

You are unique, valuable, precious, talented and wiser than you know, and it is time that the world knew it. Never let anyone, whether it be personally or professionally hold you back from becoming the 'best you' possible.

Fear never wants what is good for you, it only wants to control you.

Chapter 5:

Making Decisions for the Wrong Reasons

*REMEMBER, you alone get to choose
what matters and what doesn't. The
meaning of everything in your life has
precisely the meaning you give it.*

W e have all made decisions for the
wrong reasons. It happens and we
need to learn from it. What concerns
me is when a person, especially women, keep on
making decisions that are not good for their life.
In this chapter, I am going to share with you a
decision I made that I don't regret, but I
recognize it was made with the wrong motives.

The decision I made? To try and have a second
child. Why did I make that decision? Because the

whole family, the siblings of my ex-husband, everybody had more than two or three kids, I was the only one who had only one son, and I was always blamed that I could not conceive anymore.

To fit in, I said to myself, "Okay, what if I conceive, maybe that would create some kind of a connection between me and my ex-husband and then I will be more accepted in the family. Maybe the family won't look at me as somebody who is healthy and can't make babies. They won't label me as a sick person. I will prove them wrong and having another baby will make things right."

When I went to my doctor and said, "I want to get pregnant," and she replied, "What?" I said, "Yes, because I think I should, and I am getting older day by day, so I am not sure if I can delay it any longer and my son is eight and all alone, I need him to have siblings." I made all of these stupid reasons.

She cautioned me because my health wasn't the greatest but when she saw my determination, she gave me a diet to follow and specific things to do. I became so focused on getting pregnant because I thought that was the only solution that would make me acceptable and respectable in that family.

The worst part was in trying to fit in. I was denying that I was being hurt. I was ignoring the fact that I was not needed, and not accepted. Those things were very obvious, but I kept all those obvious things off to one side and told myself that if I had a baby this would all change. I don't know why I thought that way, but I did, and that's the wrong decision I made for myself.

Why Do Women Make Decisions For The Wrong Reasons?

Because we think that the decision will be the answer or remedy for our problem. For me, a baby was the best solution, so I conceived.

We make some very impractical and illogical perceptions and presumptions and then make decisions that are no good. Today I ask myself, "How would a baby change the perception of people that I'm sick, because even after the baby I was taking insulin injections. It's not that my diabetes will just go away. How would my husband feel that I love him more? Where would that come from? How would my way of talking to people, and the mindset that I had, change with a baby? Having another child would increase, not decrease, the objections to me working."

I was so numb inside that I didn't see the truth. I stayed in a state of denial and I am not the only one. Have you ever been in denial about a bad situation in your life? When you do, it has an impact that is internal and very damaging. You become filled with self-doubt, lack of confidence, fear and you feel yourself too little for everything. You start to thank people for hurting you and berate yourself for being who you are.

What everyone says becomes the noise that makes you numb to logic and then you make wrong decisions because of it. I honestly thought that bringing in a new family member would cause the family to bond, and it didn't.

You make decisions for wrong reasons because you think that things will improve or change. It was never my ex-husband or his family that came to me and said that if you have a second child, we will love you. It never came from them. Because they were taunting me throughout the eight years that I only had one child, I thought, "Oh, they keep telling me this because she has a career, so she doesn't want to make more babies. Maybe if I give birth to a baby, then they will say, 'Oh she's sincere.'" So, to prove my

[58]

sincerity, loyalty, commitment, I thought I would bring another member into the family. But it's the wrong decision. There was no logic behind it, to be very honest.

Now that being said, I have no regrets about having my son whatsoever. I regret how I made the decision, but my son brings so much joy to my life. He's wonderful, adorable and so much fun to be around. I can't imagine my life without him.

Stop Making Decisions For The Wrong Reasons

The first step is to recognize that you are doing it. Take responsibility for the fact that you made a mistake, that you chose the wrong path. It is hard to do, but truth is what will always set you free.

Next is to realize that you are not making decisions based on yourself but on others and external factors like, "What will this person think or what will happen if I do that?" When you do that, you hurt yourself. Decisions should not be based on how another person responds to it. It should be based on the fact that it is the right decision.

If you put it in a corporate environment, imagine if you have to make a decision and think if you say something your boss will not like, or it is not something that has happened over the years in this society, or in the company's culture and if I do it – what if they don't like it, or what if they ask me to leave?

Decisions made in fear are never the right decision. You have to trust yourself and your ability to not only survive but thrive in this world. I made the decision to have another child in the hopes that those who were supposed to love me would and it didn't work. I was still unwanted, diabetic, and outspoken and no amount of children was going to change that. That fear of staying unloved drove me to do something I wouldn't have normally done.

Third, when you have to make important decisions, examine it from all sides including emotionally. Ask yourself why you are making a certain decision and be very honest with yourself. If it is for any reason besides being the right thing to do, then you need to reconsider it.

I want to encourage you to have faith in yourself and your ability to make the right decisions for the right reasons. I now do that, and it is self-empowering. Do I make mistakes? Of course, I do, I am human. But I take responsibility for them and it always turns out okay.

Make the decision today to make careful choices and watch your life transform before your eyes.

The right help comes from the right people, only if you know what is right for yourself.

Chapter 6:

Fight For What Is Right

*Fighting for one's freedom, struggling
towards being free, is like struggling to
be a poet or a good Christian or a good
Jew or a good Muslim or good Zen
Buddhist. You work all day long and
achieve some kind of level of success by
nightfall, go to sleep and wake up the
next morning with the job still to be
done. So, you start all over again.*

Maya Angelou

When Stacey was four, her mother died
from cancer, leaving her, her sister
and her Dad Rick on their own. It was
the 1970's and no one thought that a man could
raise two girls on his own. Even some of the
family suggested that Rick should give the girls
up for adoption.

[63]

Rick thought about the request but not for long. There was no question in his mind that there was only one right thing to do. He knew it would be hard, but he could never subject his girls to a life of foster homes separated from each other hoping that someone would adopt them all the while questioning why their Dad didn't love them enough.

He kept his girls. It challenged him in ways that he could never imagine, especially as the teenage years hit and the hormones and emotions raged, but he survived. In 2003 he passed away, leaving a wonderful wife (he remarried), two daughters, two step kids and seven grandchildren who now share his legacy and love down to the next generations.

Stacey tells everyone about her wonderful Dad and how he raised her to love others and his life was the example.

It Was The Right Thing To Do

From the time I was little, I was taught to fight for what is right, and when I was kicked out of my home and going through the process of my divorce that belief was tested. I was told that I should leave my sons in Pakistan and go live my own life, that trying to get custody of them was too hard.

I was told 'He should take the responsibility', you should leave them behind and live a better and successful life. You have your whole life ahead of you.'

But the point was not about me, it was about what was right.

I have been in that misery. I have been in a culture and an atmosphere where treating women badly was normal. I never wanted my sons to be there. And the world to have another two brutal men growing up and not respecting women and not understanding the basics of human rights and freedom for every individual.

If I left them behind, I would have added to the misery that already existed, I had been with them through all of the pain and agony of chauvinism, and women not being treated right, or given respect. I had lived through those moments; I was the victim myself.

If I had left my sons behind, I would have added my stamp of approval to it. It would have been my contribution to a world of wrong-doing. The world would have another two individuals in the society who would do the same to women, who would not respect women, who would not understand that women can do better, and they are human beings as well.

[65]

The other side of it was an emotional one. My sons wanted to live with me. They didn't want to be with their father, but I was being pressured by society and the laws of the land to give them up. Leaving them would have been the easiest thing to do but the consequences were unthinkable.

Their trust would be shattered, and when people lose their element of trusting others and believing in others, they are being brutal to themselves. They become judgmental, cynical, and critical. Their personalities would have been shattered, they would have become another version of their father, and I would have been a hypocrite. How could I stand up for human rights and the rights of women and leave my two sons to grow up to be what I was fighting against?

They needed to be with me, no matter what the cost. I will raise them to respect all people and to give everyone a fair chance in life.

Why You Must Fight For What Is Right

There's no meaning in life if you are not ready to stand up and fight for what you believe in. Everyone needs to step up and say, "This is not right," and we need to work around this or an alternate, and let the world see a different perspective.

When changes are not made, things are carried from one generation to another. They become so regular and routine that we don't even realize that what we are doing is hurting the entire system and humankind.

The reason that you don't fight for what is right is fear. You are scared of how others will react. You are afraid of being judged and opposed. You don't want to stand out in a way where you will be ostracized and left alone. So, you choose not to speak up or not to fight for what is right.

But if we do that, then the misery and the pain that exists in the world stays. We chose to live in misery and just console ourselves by saying, 'It happens and there is nothing I can do about it.' My dad has lived through it, my mom has lived through it, my uncle has lived through it, our forefathers have lived through it, so, it's okay to do it this way or let it go this way.

For me, if you don't have the guts or if you don't get up to fight for what is right; you are not only killing yourself, but you are being unfair to the coming generations and to the society at large.

How To Fight For What Is Right

There are many different situations in life, from personal to professional, where you will need to stand up for yourself. For instance, if you are in a career and you feel like a team member is being left behind or not being utilized to their full potential, or maybe it is you that is not being given the right opportunities and you know that you can do more, then you need to speak up. If you feel that you are being penalized because of your sex, race or education, then you need to let others know.

All of this comes under 'fight for what is right' – so when you feel that something needs to be addressed, something needs to be changed; within your capacity, you have to step up and speak up.

The problem is when we see something going wrong in our company or in our organization, or our business, what we say is that it has been like this forever. We shouldn't be the one to change it. Let it be like this, why should I step ahead and why should I become the culprit, why should I do that?

It's not about you, it's about doing the right thing the right way. If you feel that your participation, anything that you say or do will make a positive difference in your organization, your business, handling your team, or connecting with others – you should step up and fight for it and speak up.

Let me clarify one thing, when I say fight, I don't mean yell, scream, physically touch someone or call them names. You always must fight with the best tool possible, respect. You fight through the power of your words, not how much you can hurt and bully someone. When you do that, you become just like them. In chapter ten, I am going to share many ways to overcome opposition. In this chapter, I want to focus on the fact that you need to have the courage within yourself to take those bold steps.

I want you to think about people who have changed the world to a better place. People like Martin Luther King Jr, Abraham Lincoln, and Rosa Parks. They changed a whole country and set a whole race of people free and they did it through peace and respect and not backing down. They were incredibly strong and non-violent at the same time. They endured incredibly hard things but in the end, a whole nation was changed.

Yes, they paid a big price. I am not going to lie to you and there may be a cost to doing what is right, but the rewards when those bad circumstances are changed are worth it. I paid a big price for my freedom, but it has been worth it. Every hard thing, even fearing for my life at times, has allowed me a joy I have never known before and now my story has become a part of a bigger story.

I think about diversity and inclusion. Twenty years ago, there was no such thing as diversity and inclusion. But now organizations, corporations, small and mid-size businesses, even, politics, and media, everywhere you go, everybody is talking about diversity and inclusion and taking diversity and inclusion initiatives.

Why has this happened? Because there are people who said, 'this is not right, we have to include everyone, and respect everyone regardless of their gender or their background or their culture'. We have to, because it gives a different dimension to discovery, to innovation, to growth, and to prosperity. So, it's a global world now, let's work together, let's rise together.

Let me ask you some difficult questions. Is being harmed right for you? Are you okay with people mistreating you? Are you okay having to compromise because of your gender, culture, past, color or creed? Are you ready to let people take advantage of you? Do you feel it is right that you stay in misery just because you don't have the self-confidence to fight?

There are fights at a personal level you have to do every day; you have to fight for your dreams. The voice of 'no' is strong in us. Then we hear the voice that tells us 'yes do it, try it'. So, we need to fight that battle every day.

For me, doing this book is some days a fight. There are a bunch of noises that say, "Just leave it." The moment it comes out, there may be people that are going to misjudge it, there will be people who will say it's going against typical religion, or men who don't have open-mindedness regarding women, etc.

Or it can be seen by some parts of the world as something that is revolutionizing the way that women should think about themselves and approach the world.

The voice in my head goes, "Why are you getting into this whole new pandora box after so much struggle? Now that your kids are settled and you have a job, just settle down and leave it. Just move on, go with the flow."

This noise is so loud, it comes to my mind, it talks to me, it speaks to me, it yells at me every single day. Every single day I give it a shut-up call, I fight it. I tell it that my message has to reach the world and people should know, women should know, men should know, because it is so important for both. So, it's about your own visibility and your own identity.

So, you have to fight on both ends. One fight you do that makes a larger impact, a larger difference, a visible difference, which the world can see. That is what you do when say things or step up for reasons as big as diversity and inclusion or women empowerment, or stopping domestic violence, those are the bigger issues.

Then there is the fight that you fight with your own self to make sure that you are ready to step up and fight for the world. That fight becomes more significant and is very critical for the world.

So, in concluding this chapter, remember these three things. It is always right to fight for what is right. The price is worth it. The biggest fight you will face is the one inside yourself.

In the next chapter, I share with you a vital concept to success in both life and business. DON'T WAIT!

Chapter 7:

Plan Ahead, Don't Wait

*Even at the lowest of lows, maintain a
mindset that influences you to move
forward.*

One of the lowest points on my journey to
freedom taught me one of the greatest
lessons I could learn…

When you live in countries like the US, Canada,
UK, and Australia, you have a completely
different perspective on family law and how
things work in terms of divorce and custody. As
a man or woman, you have equal rights, the
equities are supposed to be split evenly, and
custody is determined by what is best for the
child (at least in most cases).

When you live under Sharia law that is not the case. As a child, my father raised me to believe that I had the same rights as a man. That I was smart and capable of making decisions and taking responsibility.

The day we were thrown out of the house, my oldest son declared in no uncertain terms that he wanted to live with me. It was one of the proudest moments of my life but caught my husband completely off-guard. He assumed the boys would want to stay with him. That was a blow to his male ego, because what male child in Pakistan would choose to stay with his mother over his father? My son knew better because I had taught him well and he knew that his father did not care about him.

Then came the time for the divorce and I didn't realize how one-sided it was going to be. I was handed the signed divorce papers from my husband. There was no conferring ahead of time. No figuring out what was to be in those papers. He put the terms and conditions that he wanted, and I was expected to go along with it. Many of the terms didn't make sense or contradicted common sense. Some of the more interesting ones included:

> If I kept the boys their father will take them out of his will.

> He will not pay any money for their upkeep.

> He can see them whenever he wants, or the boys can see him when they want, and I could not stop him.

> I would take care of the boys and have financial responsibility for them, but he would have custody and final say on all decisions about them or he could claim custody anytime he wanted.

I had no option to change any of it. Because my ex had signed it, the judge had made it legal without any input from me. He had all the rights and I did not.

It made no sense whatsoever. So, I was to take care of the boys both physically and financially, but he had all the control. It always came back to control. He didn't care about his boys at all. He was already remarried with an obedient, young wife who would give him what he wanted. He didn't need my sons anymore.

When we lived in the same city, he never came to see them. A good father would take financial responsibility for his family. He never paid me one cent. Thankfully, I had a great job and so I didn't need his money, but it made me think of other women who were not as blessed and how they struggled.

All he wanted was to control and punish me for being an independent woman and use my boys to do it. I wasn't going to put up with it. I got a lawyer and decided to fight back.

Here is where the lowest point came. I was trying to fight Sharia law and it wasn't going to work. It didn't matter what I said or the logic of my arguments or how right I was, I am a woman and I am wrong. I showed the court that my husband didn't care about his boys, they didn't care. He would argue that I wasn't safe, and I shouldn't have them, but on the other side he didn't want them in his house. So, were they supposed to go to the orphanage? It didn't make sense. My lawyer kept trying to warn me not to speak up and not to argue, but I would and came out frustrated and hurt.

There was a point when I realized that I would never win. It's a vicious circle. I will be standing in the cold, going through my character assassination, trying to prove my worth, trying to prove how good of a mother I am or how good of a woman or a professional I am. I tried to prove my capability to raise the kids, but nobody understood.

I had a choice to make. Continue to fight and never win or look like I had given up and start to move forward anyway. I have to admit, there was a part of me that wanted to continue to fight but I had to think about what was best for my boys. The decision became easier when I thought about it that way.

The next step was to plan. It became apparent that I needed to get out of the country. The only way I would be free was to remove myself from where he had control. Could I do it? If I failed, I would lose everything, possibly my life. If my husband found out, he had the influence to have me killed and legally there was nothing I could do to stop him.

My first move was to Dubai with my kids, but I forgot that Dubai is also a Muslim country, so when I went there my kids were not given admission to school because they were asking for their custody certification. The mother cannot have custody of the boys, and if I had them, there must be a certificate or an approved signed paper from the father stating that they can live with me and I can put them in school.

[77]

But I didn't have that paper, so, the admissions were denied. They were unable to get admitted to a school. Under those circumstances, I had to send my sons back to Pakistan to continue their education. I couldn't go back because a lot had been invested in this relocation.

So, I sent my kids back to Pakistan. I arranged domestic support for them, a maid, a driver, etc. to help them go through the daily work and attend school and everything. I was visiting them every fifteen days and I realized this is not working because the boys are not safe there.

Their father can use this against me. They are at the mercy of their domestic staff and there's nobody there. He could say she's travelling and she's not around and she just visits them once a week, and I knew that everything would go against me. What am I supposed to do? At this point, my first plan had failed, and I didn't know what to do but God had different plans for me, and I will share that story with you in the next chapter.

You Must Always Have A Plan

If I had waited for the law to change for me, for people to have sympathy for me and my boys, or the mind of my husband to change, or some kind of a miracle to happen, I wouldn't have reached this point. My kids wouldn't have been safe at all.

So, instead of waiting, I tried my best. When you are stuck in a situation try your best to work through it, but when you are in a situation and you are trying to work through it, you will have the analysis and the data in front of you to decide whether waiting is the answer. Or you need to take steps right now to work on bigger dangers and bigger problems.

What you do then is you step up, and that's the point when everything is going against you. Instead of giving up to failure, giving yourself to failures, start planning to get yourself out of the situation.

You cannot just sit and say 'okay it's not working, and I'm a failure now nothing can happen'; that's the wrong approach. Martin Luther King started a movement with a speech that was all about dreams. But then if we want to win that dream, achieve that dream, it has to be backed by a plan.

It is very important when you are making big decisions in your life, whether it's about your business or your personal life, to plan things for yourself and everything that you do. If you are not planning, you are making life difficult for yourself.

When I was thrown out of the house, I was trying to make everything happen, for the first six months. Sending them to school, getting things available for them in terms of food, provide toys for the little one. It was a fight for me. I struggled.

The moment I decided to focus on taking full custody of my sons, it gave me the spirit and energy to fight. Because then I had a plan. I would not abandon my two boys to be raised as ruthless, uncaring men.

Sometimes life tries to throw you curve-balls. It is up to you how you deal with them. You can let them take you out or you can put a plan in place to deal with them. Once you have that plan, then it is time for action.

If I had waited, there was a good possibility that I would not have my sons today. Every day that you wait puts your dreams at risk. Don't risk losing what is precious to you because you stall and don't move forward. It may be hard, but I can guarantee that it is worth it.

Chapter 8:

Look For Those Who Will Help You

The strong individual is the one who asks for help when they need it.

Rona Barrett

I wouldn't be where I am today unless I had asked for help from the right people. I call them partners in believing. They believed in me and knew that the only way to make a good life for my boys was for me to leave the country.

There are also those who pretended to help me but were only out for their selfish gain. My lawyer was one of them. Because I left my kids behind, I always had this fear that my ex-husband would try to use it against me and tell the court that I am not there to take care of the kids, and the kids are not safe. Which is what he had started to do. He painted me as an irresponsible, career-oriented woman who didn't care about her kids.

When that happened, I realized that fighting this case will end up nowhere; the kids will be in pain, there will always be something disturbing them, and then the insecurity that was going around me was both mentally and emotionally too much.

So, I spoke to my lawyer, and I said, "Give me the real picture. Will I be able to get the custody for sure or not?" He didn't want to tell me the truth that I couldn't win because he would be out of money.

Instead, he said, "To keep on trying, you have a strong financial background, you have a solid job and are educated. You haven't taken any money from him until now; in terms of alimony or kids' expenses or anything of that sort. He doesn't come and see the kids." He was bringing up all of those points and said that you still have a strong case, don't give up and let's fight.

I felt, something deep inside me that said, "It's not true." Had it been true, something would have happened that was positive up to now. We

[82]

were showing the court these things and it hadn't made any difference at all.

If we were already doing these things and nothing was happening, then how was it going to change in a couple of weeks or months?

At that moment I had a conversation with myself where I told myself, "To pause, Nageen, and listen. It may be hard on you, but you are fighting for something that will not happen in this country. It will be years and years of waiting and your children will grow up in that weird environment, always struggling."

I accepted my loss and surrendered. I did not give up, I surrendered to the fact that it's not going to happen. I shifted to reality, to something that was practical.

It was also a sign for me to get some support, because now what? I knew that I was not going to get custody of my boys here, and I didn't want this to continue. I wanted a better life for myself and my kids, and to make sure that my kids had a secure life. What do I do now?

Then I reached out – the lesson here is the moment you surrender to the facts and you understand them, and then it's like something opens up and you want to try to figure out

[83]

things in a different perspective. Instead of knocking on the closed door, again and again, you start to figure out what comes next.

What do I have available to me right now that can help me? I knew that the company that I worked for has 32 offices worldwide, and I said, "What if I take my kids out of here?" Take them out and they will stay with me because everything is dependent upon my job. If I don't have a job in Pakistan, then the kids can't stay here – obviously, they are going to go with me. Let me try this angle.

I did not discuss this with my lawyer at all, because I know he wouldn't have supported me. So, I went to my boss and I discussed what was going on and that I wanted to be relocated. He said that he was going to review it, obviously he can't decide right away, but said he was going to discuss it with the people in HR given the circumstances that I am in, and he would get back to me.

The HR personnel came to me and said, 'where do you want to go?' I thought because Dubai was the closest place and there's not a big cultural change and there aren't so many requirements for Pakistani nationals to move there, it's always easy, that was my impression.

[84]

Of course, you know from the last chapter going to Dubai was not a good choice and now I was in a situation again. Even during that time when my boys were in Pakistan, there were people who helped me, especially the school the boys had originally gone to. I went to them to see if the boys could get back in there even though they had missed over three months of school. They could have easily said no, but they welcomed the boys back and helped them get on track, which helped a lot, but I still didn't know what I was going to do next.

Here is one thing I have learned. When you need help, ask for it. I asked God to help me and open a door for me and He did it in a most unexpected way.

A Big Change Was Coming

I have an incredible friend, more like a soul mate who now lives in the US after immigrating from Pakistan many years ago. I called him and told him what had happened in Dubai, now the kids are in Karachi and I'm in Dubai and I don't know what to do. He said, "Why don't you come to the U.S.?"

My first response was, "No I can't," and he said, "Why?" I told him that there was no way for me to get a visa for the kids because I don't have the letter from my ex-husband. It's been declared that I am a divorcee and they will check for that.

The words he spoke next changed my life forever. He said, "What if they don't ask for the custody papers? I was annoyed and ended the conversation, but his words kept rattling around in my brain. I couldn't let them go. I knew deep down that I had to try.

I applied for the tourist visa for my kids to the U.S. and my oldest son was called to go for an interview. I already had a U.S. visa because I was travelling back and forth already for business reasons.

When we got there, the Visa Officer just looked at me, the papers and my son, and asked how old he was, and he said, "I'm twelve." "Oh, you are so tall for a twelve-year-old," and they exchanged smiles.

Then she asked whether the kids have ever travelled with me outside of Pakistan, and I said, "Yeah, they've been with me because I used to take them on trips to places where it's easier to go." She could see that on the passport.

You know what her answer was? Here are your visas. I was frozen. I didn't know what to think. I stepped out of there thinking, "She didn't even ask me about that custody paper." Something happened; an external, a larger help came to us and that lady didn't even ask about that. So, it was just a tourist visa with the mom, and that's about it. To this day I still wonder why she didn't ask about the custody papers.

The lesson here is that if you don't take the risk, you have already failed. Just because you think the answer will be no, why wouldn't you try, because you don't know. Don't consider yourself all-knowing. You don't have all of the answers. You step ahead and ask and try. It's a risk, but the answers will come.

In the next chapter, I am going to tell you about the trip from Pakistan to the US. It is a powerful story of how to overcome fear in your life as we ran for ours. We did make it to the U.S., and we arrived on Mother's Day. It was very symbolic to me because I got my children to a safe place.

I did not even share with my boss or the two or three people that had helped me throughout, that I was moving. I told them that I needed a week off.

When I was in the U.S., I checked in with my company and I told them I was in the U.S. with my kids. They couldn't believe it. I told them I wanted to start a new life. They were supportive but concerned because I didn't have a work visa. They stepped up to help me. I had left them with no notice, and they were still there for me. They understood my situation and came alongside me to get me what I needed to provide for me and my boys.

Normally, the H-1 Visa covers family also, but in my case, the children are under age and I did not have custody papers for them, which is not a U.S. law requirement. However, it is a prerequisite of the law of the land where they are coming from, and they are citizens of Pakistan.

I could get a work visa, but the kids would have to go back to Pakistan. That was not going to happen. I knew that there had to be a solution and again I reached out for help. My friend, my soulmate "Rashid" guided me through the process of filing asylum or refugee status for the boys and I did.

Guess what? Within a week it was accepted because we filed genuine papers and told the truth. I needed a safe place to raise my boys and they agreed. Now, not only could my boys stay in the U.S., but they could go to school and had medical insurance. I also received my work authorization which enabled me to work legally.

By now I have consumed a major chunk of my savings and with just a few thousand dollars, I started my life again. It was not easy for my kids nor for me to adopt a lifestyle that was completely in contrast to the luxurious life that we have been living all of our lives in Pakistan. As a family, we believed that this too shall pass, and we were thankful that even if we struggled financially, we are safe and with honesty and hard work, we will regain our lost prestige. All I can say is, "God is good to those who believe in Him."

Don't Do It Alone

My advice to everyone is that you must have your partners in believing. When you are feeling weak or when you are surrendering yourself to some facts which may not be positive and powerful, or it looks like you may be losing in life, you need support. It's normal, we are human, and we need support. You can reach out to people; the right help comes from the right people if you know what is right for yourself.

If you are aligned with your core values, you know exactly what you need – in my case it was not my intention to be settled in the U.S but only to find a safe haven for myself and my kids where we could not only survive but thrive. I am very, very thankful, and blessed and grateful that it happened because we are getting a better life and have not compromised on being ethical and fair.

Chapter 9:

Never Let Fear Stop You

*I learned that courage was not the
absence of fear, but the triumph over it.
The brave man is not he who does not
feel afraid, but he who conquers that
fear.*

Nelson Mandala

Can I admit something to you? Fear was
the constant enemy that I had to fight
since the day my ex-husband kicked me
out. After years of abuse, my self-confidence was
not where it should be, and fear tried to take
advantage of the situation.

You need to hear the truth. Fear is not your
friend. He pretends to be. He comes alongside
you and whispers in your ear the excuses you
want to hear to keep you from living your

dream. He sounds like he is concerned for your safety and well-being. His voice is smooth and welcoming, and the temptation will be to listen to that voice and give in. Once you do, he has won.

If you don't listen at first, he will up the game and start telling you everything that can go wrong, from the smallest thing to the most insane idea possible. Anything to keep you from taking that step of faith.

Then if you don't listen to that voice, he will bring others in to confirm that what he said was right. Fear never wants what is good for you, he only wants to control you.

What about all the things we should be afraid of, like standing at the top of a tall building and falling off or being careful to cross a busy street? I have two words for that – common sense. If we act with common sense to avoid real potential dangers, we should never have to fear at all.

The Fears I Conquered

I want to be open and honest with you about fear. It is one of the major obstacles that holds you back from becoming the 'best you' and accomplishing things you never thought possible.

On the TV show Star Trek Voyager, in the episode The Thaw, Katherine Janeway has to deal with a personification of fear that is holding some of her crew and others hostage and killing them off slowly. She outwits fear and as he starts to disappear, Katherine says to him, "You know as well as I do, that fear only exists for one purpose – to be conquered."

I have learned how to conquer my fear and by sharing it with you here I hope that you will have the courage to conquer yours too.

When my sons and I were preparing to leave to come to the U.S. I kept everything secret. No one knew where we were going, including the people at work. I bought tickets to Dubai first and then the U.S., to make it look like we were going on a vacation.

Even though my ex-husband did not care at all about his sons and had not even seen them, let alone provide any support for them, he loved to torture me. Given the opportunity to hurt me, he would. I was a constant reminder of his biggest failure to convert me into a proper woman under Sharia law. There were things he had changed on the outside, but he knew on the inside I still knew him for who he was; a coward and a bully hiding behind his money, influence and the law.

[93]

Because of that, I was terrified that if he found out I was taking the boys out of his control, he would come to snatch them or get someone else to abduct them for him. He was rich and influential, and I was a woman with no rights. We were escaping for our lives.

I am not trying to be melodramatic, but it was the truth. My ex-husband could have me killed there and no one would even blink. Leaving Pakistan with my sons was one of the hardest things I have ever done. Fear whispered all these bad things that could happen, and I had to fight each one. I had to tell that voice in my head to shut-up regularly. If I was to give my boys a good life, we had to leave and not a single person could know, so that it did not get back to their father.

There were many other fears, two of the biggest ones were, "Could I do this on my own?" and "What about my career?" What would happen when work found out that I had moved to another country without telling them? Would they drop me, and I would be starting over, or would they help me? I didn't know and I couldn't risk telling them for fear someone would say the wrong thing and it would get back to my ex-husband.

I couldn't let those thoughts derail me. I had to push through and not give up on my goal of having a safe place for me and my boys to live. This is the decision I made stepping out of fear and doubt, and so I knew I would win.

Thankfully, when I got to the States my company understood and was gracious enough to take me back on board as a full-time employee. I had to compromise on my leadership role because they didn't have anything at that time to offer me equivalent to what I was in Pakistan.

Once I got my work authorization I had to work, otherwise how would I support us? My office was taking me back and that was the best thing to do but it came at the sacrifice of everything I had built career-wise over the last twenty years. The compromise on my career had shattered me deeply. This was the career I had created for myself in spite of all the odds and restrictions from my in-laws and husband. Today I had to let go of all that I had earned to get prepared for a new and more promising future for my boys. It was like amputating a leg or an arm to keep yourself alive.

That was very hard, and I cried many nights, but it has been worth it.

Then arriving in the U.S., how were we going to adapt? I still had some money, but the culture was completely different from any I had known, and we wouldn't be living in the lifestyle we had before. How would my boys accept life and how would the U.S. accept them? Simple things like where would we live, would I be able to buy a car, all these things weighed down on me in the form of fear.

I was also going to have to do this alone without any support. In Pakistan, I had friends and family; here other than my childhood friend, there would be none and will it be fair to put him through my tough journey? Was I strong enough to do this?

Most of my fears had to do with me and my ability to make this happen. Was I capable enough?

The answer is yes and so are you!

How To Conquer Fear

I personally feel that when you fear it creates a ripple effect on everything that you do.

Every time you fear, you are holding yourself from getting anything better out of life, or from exploring an avenue of your own self which can be a masterpiece. Or maybe it can lead you to something bigger.

Fear, shame, guilt, anger; they all stop you from love, joy, peace, gratitude, and success.

If you have limiting beliefs in your subconscious mind, you are not ready to accept that you can do something you fear. Then you start giving up. You don't even try because you don't want to take the risk.

Can I share a secret with you? You manifest what you believe. You don't manifest what you want. You may want a big house, but if you don't believe subconsciously that you can have it or that you are worthy of it, it will never happen.

You need to reprogram your mindset. One of the best questions I have learned to ask myself is - What is the best that could happen?

In my case, the fear was stopping me to apply for a U.S. visa for my kids. The fear and the doubt about being not accepted were stopping me. But when my friend said, "What if they do?" It was life-changing for me. Those four words caused a complete mindset shift. It took me from the realm of fear to the realm of possibilities.

Now it is your turn. What fears are holding you back from achieving your goals and dreams?

[97]

Look at them, study them and determine first of all if they are real? Most fears are not.

Secondly, what if it doesn't turn out the best? What if it only turns out to be 90% of what you want, is it worth it? Third, take action. You will never know what is possible until you start to move forward.

Never let fear stop you from living life to the fullest. You will be amazed at how wonderful life can become and the support group that the universe will create for you when fear is not your friend anymore!

Chapter 10:

There Will Always be Opposition

Just as we develop our physical muscles through overcoming opposition - such as lifting weights - we develop our character muscles by overcoming challenges and adversity.

Steven Covey

No one goes through life without opposition. It is necessary to pause to see what is on the inside of you and refine yourself, so that you can become a better person that is ready for bigger things.

That doesn't mean that you should go looking for opposition, but when it comes, you need to be ready for it, learn the lessons it has to teach you, and then get out of it.

I am so thankful for my dad. What he instilled in me allowed me not only to endure but grow stronger through the opposition. The biggest lesson that my dad taught me is that you have to be truthful. Always speak the truth and never make compromises on the right thing. Your integrity is imperative, no matter what. Growing up, seeing him practice this to the fullest, instilled deep inside of me how valuable it is.

My marriage was a different story. I could see variations and differences between what they were saying, what they were doing, and what they believed in.

When it comes to integrity, the things that began happening to us after the divorce were also in contrast to those values. My ex-husband only wanted custody of the boys to punish me and prove that he was the man in his culture and had control over me. He didn't care about his boys and that became evident when he didn't contribute financially, nor spend time with them.

Taking a Risk Against The Odds

The moment I realized that the divorce case was not going anywhere, and it had now become more of a male chauvinism and ego situation than anything else, I knew that it was time to quit struggling and do something different. He had his new wife and kids and now I needed to see where my life with the boys needed to go.

Accepting your failure (or as I like to call them, growth opportunities) saves you from wasting your mental, physical, emotional, and financial energies. It prevents you from going into anger, depression and blaming yourself. It is easy to get into thoughts like "I'm not good enough. Why me?' or 'I'm hopeless'. When you can accept what happened, it allows you to let it go, frees you to dream new dreams, and fuels you to explore new possibilities.

As you know from previous chapters, I ended up in the US with my boys.

When I got here, I was given some options. The first option was that my office could give me a work visa. But, if I got that visa, my kids would have to go back, because the paperwork required me to produce custody papers that I could not do.

My family and friends advised me that I had made the biggest mistake of my life. Why am I taking the burden of raising these boys, when their father is not even concerned and responsible for them? Send them back to their father, tell him that these are his kids, and get settled in the USA with a company-sponsored work visa and advance my career. Focus on your own life.

For me, it is a matter of integrity and love. I replied, "Why did I start all of this in the first place? I did not go to the U.S. because I wanted to improve my career. I went because I wanted to have a safe place for my boys. If I sent my boys back, that whole idea would have just gone down the drain. I love them with all my heart. I am not giving them up!"

How could I give them up? They were MY boys. Even if I did want to give them up, how could I send them back to a man who did not love them; a dishonorable man whom I could not trust? It was not happening.

After I told them that, they labelled me as an emotional person who doesn't see things with practical eyes. I didn't care, my boys are worth it.

I spoke to my friend and his lawyer to check on other legal options. I was advised to take asylum or refugee status in the U.S. They informed me that there is a risk involved in this. If I submitted my application to acquire an asylum or a refugee status, there was a possibility that it can get rejected. If it gets rejected, then I would have to go back to my country with the boys within the time specified by the immigration judge, and my current visa (a visit visa of five years) would no longer be valid.

I knew I did not have a choice, so I took the risk. I was so sure that I could get it with the papers I had and with what I had already gone through. I went to the immigration website again and again, and I read about what kind of people could apply and what type of paperwork was needed. I was cross-checking and working every end of it.

At the same time, people were telling me to marry a US citizen instead of claiming refugee status. My kids and I could get a green card in six months.

This was not an option for me. I was here to save my kids. I was not over the mental, physical and emotional trauma of my previous marriage. Now they were telling me to marry another person and make his life miserable with the agenda that this person will get us U.S. citizenship? What if he doesn't accept my kids? What if he isn't a good father? Most importantly, what if he was another man of the same DNA my ex-husband was? I was so upset. Even today, when I think about this advice and those words, the hurt comes up.

I realized that listening to all that opposition was hurting me, so I shut myself off from all that noise and decided to move forward and see what happens. Worst case, I thought, I will go back to Pakistan, and if I do go back, maybe I will try to go to a different city. I did not know how things would work, but I told myself to give it a try.

The Right Path is Not Always Easy

I did not want to give up the right path just because it was difficult. I spoke to my office about it and told them this was what I was doing. They were open and told me that I wouldn't be able to work for them until I got my acceptance because I wouldn't have work authorization. Because of that, I knew that I would have to survive for another three to six months, providing I got accepted, before my work authorization came in.

Despite all of this, I still believed in trying and seeing what would happen. I had already made decisions like getting pregnant for the second time, because I had thought it would make me more acceptable. I had learned my lesson. I said,

"No. Let me do it the other way. Let me take the right path and do what is right."

So, the application went in. Within a week, I sent all the documents I had, even the ones that weren't listed. I had all of the reports, the core papers, and other paperwork, and I put it all together and sent it. Within a week, we got a letter from immigration telling us our case was filed, and we could stay in the U.S. until the hearing. After that, they asked us to do fingerprinting, photographs, blood tests, and other legal stuff, so they could get us into the immigration database.

I applied for my work authorization, which took around three or four months. During that time, I was jobless. However, I knew that when it did come, I could go back to my job. I focused on the positive things and did not allow my brain to travel down the road of 'What if?'

Those four months were financially and emotionally hard for us. I had come from a senior-level position where I was frequently traveling around. Just being home and hoping that things would change was difficult for me, but it was the right thing to do. My kids were amazing. They ate what I could afford and wore what I could buy. They hugged me more often and did extremely well in their schools. Their exceptional school grades would give me the assurance that I was on the right path.

Stay True to Yourself

I strongly believe that you have to be committed to yourself and be true to your purpose. You need to make sure that your values, your words, and your approach to life are not compromised.

I could sit around and do nothing, or I could take action, but what action to take? When you are in situations like that it is important to listen to your inner voice.

During the period when I was jobless, my friend advised me to use my professional expertise and visit the local Chamber of Commerce to see if I can help them. Immediately, I knew inside of me that this was the course of action for me.

I offered to help guide local businesses around strategies to scale up their profits or even offer a complete road map to aspiring entrepreneurs. I built an audience around myself, a fan club while working as a volunteer. I was invited to share my story of resilience & sacrifice at the Annual Women's Leadership Conference. It led me to numerous speaking events and taught me to stand on the shoulders of my story with grace.

It was those events and watching how it changed people's lives that encouraged me to write this book. I want millions of people to know that life can be hard, your own people will stand against you, you will be betrayed, and your name will be dragged in the mud, but nothing can stop you from winning and shining.

Another volunteer job I took was at the local refugee center to teach English to female refugees. This was an effort to help them get connected with the community faster and even start jobs to support their families and become self-sufficient. None of us could go back and re-write their stories of escape from war-zone areas but we all want to help them regain their integrity and start a new life.

Due to my rising popularity from the local chamber for my volunteer work, my friend encouraged me to start my own company. I started delivering vision board and leadership workshops and also taught branding and marketing for existing and new businesses. I was wanting to give, and a door of opportunity opened for me.

Remember, grit, grace, and gratitude garners glory.

You Always Have a Purpose

From all of this, there is a lesson that God wanted me to do something. There is a purpose that I'm here. I found that purpose in the worst and darkest time of my life.

Those four months, when I was worried about what and how to feed my kids and how to clothe them was a testing time. I had run out of my savings, and everything was gone. The last bit of savings I did have, I put into my rent and basic necessities. Everything was a struggle.

Our first Thanksgiving here was the hardest. When my younger son came home from school and told me that everyone was giving gifts to their friends and teachers, and asked me if he could do that, I cried the whole night. I couldn't even spare $20 to give him for that. I was counting every single penny, but I knew that I had to do something. So, I took him to the dollar store and bought a pack of 10 cards for $2.00. I made him write those cards and decorate the envelopes. I taught him the power of love and being genuine.

My friend tried to help me as much as he could, but the truth is that my heart was bleeding deep inside because I had never imagined that taking the right path would leave me broke.

[108]

By always being truthful and living in integrity, God was able to open doors for me.

People started appreciating me. I was being referred to do different jobs for them, such as marketing and branding. I started writing fearlessly and was invited to speak at different events. These were good things coming.

My friend supported me to form my company, Nyn's Dreams. www.nynsdreams.com My dream is to help other peoples' dreams come true.

When I formed the company, I knew I had to do a website and other marketing collateral, but I had no money to do any of this. My friend gave his credit card to buy a domain, but I still wasn't sure. My friend also approached a very seasoned website designer and asked him if he can help me with my website and other graphic needs. This gentleman 'Lantz Preg' stepped in and built the entire Nyn's Dreams website and never charged me. Even when I started making money, I kept going back and asking him what I owed him. He told me, "No. I did it for a woman who is so joyful and so committed. If you are doing something for this community, for the world, let me be a little part of it. This is the least I could do."

[109]

After this, it all started happening. I started going to conferences where we needed flyers and had them done by this designer. My friend covered the charges for printing. They all did this because they were helping someone that they knew was true to her purpose. This is the kind of help that came to me.

Nobody would do this for someone that does not have a true purpose. What I have figured out from this whole situation is that God puts you in a position where He knows what the outcome is. He knows that you will be able to pass through this test. That is why He puts you there.

People say to me, "So what do you call your divorce? Is it a failure? What do you call coming here, leaving your career and your life for your kids? Isn't it a failure? How can you say it is a success?"

My answer to them is, "No". You are all looking at phases. You are not looking at the end result. God was preparing me for something big. The reason I survived major heart surgery was only because God wanted me to find my purpose and part of that was writing this book. Not only women but men also will read this book and find their true selves.

If you are on the right path, if you know what you are doing, and if you are truthful and you don't make compromises, you will get there. Opposition comes. It is what you do with it that determines your future!

Grit
grace &
gratitude
garners
glory.

Chapter 11:

Always be Truthful, Live With Integrity

*The foundation stones for a balanced
success are honesty, character, integrity,
faith, love and loyalty.*

Zig Ziglar

My role model from day one was my dad. Whatever I am today, whatever values I have, it is because of him. I saw him live by those values. He encouraged me to read the Bible and the Gita also other than our holy book Quran.

In Pakistan, if you are a Christian, or a Hindu, or any religion that isn't Muslim, and you go and visit someone's house, people are reluctant to serve you food in the same dishes that they regularly use.

I never knew about that because I did not grow up in that type of environment. Once, I went to a friend's house, and our Hindu friend, Usha, was with us. I remember my friend's mom telling her son to, "Keep the plate Usha has used separate." When I asked my friend why, she said, "Oh, because she's not Muslim. So my mom will wash them separately, and then she will purify them."

After that, I didn't enjoy the rest of the evening because I was thinking about this. I had never seen that before, and never heard of it at my house. I wasn't even aware of this ritual.

When I asked my father about it later, he told me to read the Bible and the Gita. At first, it was hard until he bought me the simpler versions. When I asked him why I had to read it, he said, "Just do it for the sake of reading it." I read it as a storybook. That is how I read the Quran in the beginning as well. It was just like going through a story in the Bible and then going through a story in Gita.

After a month or so, my dad asked if I was finished. When I said, "Yes," he asked me, "Okay, so in any of the books, you just read, did

[114]

any of them say that you should hate any human or living being?" I said, "No."

Then he said, "Okay. What were the main lessons you learned?" I replied, "It was about commitment, truthfulness, and miracles that happen to good people and all that stuff." He said, "So, everything is the same, right?" I said, "Yes."

My dad then told me, "Just keep this in mind. That is your lesson for life. Everything is the same. All religions are the same, and they teach the same message. There is only one God, but the ways to God may be different. People can take detours. Some people can fly, some can swim, some will take a boat, and those are the ways people go, but there is one God, and that is where everybody goes. So just forget about everything else."

I asked why he made me read all of this stuff. He said, "You came and asked me such a silly question about your friend's mom washing plates separately. She didn't have the exposure to other religions. She thinks that she is superior because her religion is the only one that matters."

If you haven't tasted anything else, how can you comment on that? I wanted you to have the answer yourself, instead of me guiding you to what is right or what is wrong. Now, do you think that you should put your plate separate, or not be friends with a non-Muslim? The only thing that you should hate is hatred itself. That is it, and somebody who isn't truthful."

Breaking Free From Negativity

I was brought up in the type of culture where my father helped me learn things for myself.

When I got married and had kids, there was so much negativity around me. Women were treated differently, and Islam was the only religion allowed. With all of that going around, I didn't want my boys to accept that. I sent them to a different school away from all their cousins, even though it was expensive. I paid for it myself because my husband did not believe it was a necessary expense and said I did not have a good enough reason to send them there.

I picked a school that would teach them values. They would learn to respect women and other human beings, and it was not the same culture. This school was associated with the British & American systems of education, so they had a more diverse culture. I really wanted them to get that exposure and not develop a superiority complex because they are Muslim or rich, and to learn not to be judgemental of others. Putting my kids in the right school was my first step to putting them on the right path.

I never, ever told my kids that their father was a bad person, and I never told them that he and his family do not have the right culture. Not once did I speak to them along those lines. Their father would beat me and abuse me in front of them, but I would just push him away and did not speak of it. Even when we were fighting in court, I would not allow the kids to be in the room when this was discussed.

I was a living example and role model for them and as they grew, I knew that their common sense would see what is right and what is wrong.

When my older son made the decision to stay with me, that was powerful. Not only did it reflect the love he had for me, but it went beyond that. By the age of twelve, he had understood what is right and what is wrong.

Sending The Right Message For Our Children

When I made the decision to come to the U.S., my children were looking to me for guidance. If I took a wrong step at any time or made an unhealthy compromise, my children would have gotten the wrong message. They would have seen that it is okay to manipulate things, to lie, or to say bad things about people whether or not they have said bad things about you.

My older son knew that my family was telling me to send them back to their father. When we had a conversation about it, I told him, "Look, everybody has a limited vision toward hate. It is very easy for anybody to give advice to others, but when it comes to themselves, it would be different. Let's look at it from a different perspective. Let's not say they are bad. Instead, let us say that they are programmed not to see things from a broader perspective."

It was also important for me to tell him that whatever hatred my family had, it was towards their father and not towards my kids. I told him that it was their way of protecting me because they are selfish and thinking about their own needs. It was not a justification for what they said, but I told him, "People have different perceptions. You will always remember that my mom's family always wanted you to go back to your father, and I will always remember that they were not there when I needed them the most. I will also remember that they gave me the wrong advice to send my kids back or get married again." It's all a different perception of the same thing and how you are taking it.

I had this conversation with my son, and I said that this is what diversity is. It is what thinking over freedom is all about, and that everybody has their own reasons. They will never accept that whatever they have done is wrong because they have their own reasons for doing it. In their minds, they are right. Instead of being judgemental, leave them if you can't accept it. Leave them, and you will not create the walls of hatred.

These are the kinds of conversations I have with my kids from time to time, even to this day. At the same time, I am practicing what I preach.

I don't talk about their father. Never once have I told my sons that their father never helped us pay for their school, or that something is because of their Dad. I am past that phase. We do not have to go back to the past every five minutes. That is not the way to move on.

There were times I said very little because I had this feeling that the wounded, bleeding, hurt woman inside of me would say something that would become engraved in their little souls. It became so much of me that, now, I don't even

[119]

talk about them for any reason and the kids don't remember.

They also don't question because they're busy. There's so much more they have to do in their lives than sitting and talking about people who haven't cared about them.

I see it coming out in so many ways. My younger son wants to be a cop. When I ask him why he wants to be a cop, his reply is, "Because I want to help people." In school, he is a truthful student. Something happened in the class that the children were scared to tell the principal. He knew that he would be suffering consequences by going against the other kids, but he stood up and spoke the truth. This is what I worked for. My children are my legacy.

The Value of Integrity

I teach my boys to take responsibility for their actions and results. There is no such thing as failure, and you are not allowed to blame others for poor results. For example, if your teacher gives you a low mark, for whatever reason, maybe he is racist, or he thought that you are not the right person. Do not come and tell me that you got a lower mark because the teacher gave you a lower mark. No, you got a low mark. Accept it.

In my university and college days, there were times when I was not assigned projects because I was a girl and I would fight them. I used to tell my dad, "It's not happening. These people put me on the stupid projects because I'm a girl, and they don't give me the good projects." He would say, "Okay, what do you want to do?" I would tell him, "I want to write an article. A bold article." He would tell me, "Okay, and if your college is not doing it, if they think that your incapable, prove it to them."

He took me to visit women in jail, and told me, "Take interviews. You wanted to write a bold article. Do it. Your university was not ready to send you because you are a woman. In this culture, it's not right for you to go. But I'm your father, and I'm helping you. You go, you write it. Write your article, submit it to your teacher, and let's see what happens."

In the end, my article won an award at the university. I learned that part of integrity was valuing myself. Now, I have the opportunity to pass on the lessons my dad taught me and be a good role model for my boys.

One thing I know for sure is that if I teach them the power of truth, integrity, kindness, and fairness and instill these values deeply into their hearts, they will be successful no matter what happens.

This is what my father did. He gave me these four or five values, and then I made my way. Today, I tell my kids, "There were days when we didn't have enough food, but now when we have enough, what are we supposed to do?" Both of my sons will invite their friends to our house. It is a very welcoming house with them, their friends, and their friends' families.

It is a way of giving back to the community and giving back to people who have been there for you, and your friends who love you selflessly. They don't know what your background is, whether you're a Muslim or single parent kid, or whatever else. They just love you for what you are. You have to be strong. Don't let consequences, incidents, or events define you.

My dad told me something once that I love to this day. He said, "The apple does not fall far from the tree." It is so true. The values that you teach your kids is their reality. Even if they stray from your values a bit, they will come back to it because something deep inside will bother them.

During the twelve years of my abusive marriage, I was tempted every day to stop living in integrity and not stand up for what is right. I felt like I was dying inside but I would not give up my integrity and treated everyone with value.

Keep the Doors of Communication Open

If you want your children to live their values, you need to keep communication open. They need to be able to talk to you about what is going on in their lives and the challenges they face and get your feedback.

If you can't say anything positive, don't feed the negative. If I cannot say anything positive about anyone, I do not have the right to say anything negative as well. No matter what has happened to me, it does not give me the right to pass my hatred onto others.

My Legacy

I have made mistakes. At times, I feel that I am not what I should be, but I try my best. If I don't want my kids to do something, I make sure that I do not do that thing. If I don't want them to lie, then I don't lie. If I want them to communicate, to express themselves, then I do that. If I want them to take the right path, no matter how difficult it is, I do that and continue to do till today.

That's the legacy that I want to leave behind. All I can say is that my boys will remember that mama tried. Even when she was tired, even when she was stressed. I hope they will know all I did for them. That I had every intention to be great, good and grand but some days all I could be was okay. I want my kids to remember me as a woman who fought with every ounce of her strength for what she believed was right, and from that, they will have the lesson of their life.

Chapter 12:

You Have a Purpose

*The two most important days in your life
are the day you are born and the day
you find out why.*

Mark Twain

Settling into the U.S. was a blessing and
stressful at the same time. I started to feel
that the boys and I were finally safe, but I
came here with nothing. After everything I had
been through, I was afraid of starting from
scratch. At times the number of decisions I had
to make overwhelmed me.

I remember going into the kitchen looking for a
pizza cutter, and we didn't have one. I had
always taken the pizza cutter for granted. The
thought of having to buy one left me in dread. I

[125]

had to keep telling myself, "I can do this. I am okay."

Keeping it Together on The Outside When The Inside Hurts

On the outside, no one could tell what was going on inside me. Most days I wanted to quit but knew I couldn't. I had brought my boys to the U.S. and I could not let them see me fall apart and quit. I put on a strong face both physically and emotionally.

At the office, I showed up with the most strength because my job was providing the financial support I needed. I kept all of my emotions and my mental strength intact to make sure I was delivering the standards that were expected of me.

I was working with the kids all the time. They could see that a lot was happening. It was really important to make sure that everything was in place, and that I was doing the best that could be done for them. I would take them on outings and tried to give them everything I could.

If you can learn anything from me, learn this. You are stronger than you think. No matter what you are going through, you can not only survive but thrive as I was soon to realize.

All the years of standing up to the abuse, and now being the sole parent in a new country was the last straw for my body. Just when I thought things were going good, the stress finally caught up to me…

The Day it All Came Crashing Down

On July 11, two months after arriving in the U.S. I was rushed to the hospital.

I was talking to my kids and my friends when I began to complain that I was feeling uncomfortable and that I couldn't breathe. Then, I started sweating. Everyone told me they should take me to the hospital, but I said no. I'm a diabetic, so I thought maybe my blood sugar levels had fluctuated. I said, "Let me work on that."

Deep down, I knew that something bigger was happening inside of me. I was telling my friends and kids that I was okay, because pretending to be healthy was a kind of default setting in me for so many years. Even though I was feeling physically stressed and I could feel the pain in my chest, and the breathlessness was starting to suffocate me, I told everyone I was fine.

Eventually, I couldn't take it anymore and I was rushed to the hospital. When I got there, the doctors told me that 60% of the left side of my heart was damaged. My blood pressure was unbelievably high. God was merciful in my stubbornness.

They rushed me into intensive care and started running tests. Then they started giving me injections. After that, I don't remember anything.

It took about 24 to 30 hours to stabilize me. When I did come to consciousness, the doctor told me I had to have surgery if I wanted to live and they were going to do it once I was stable enough.

Turning a Negative Into a Positive

I still remember the day I was taken in for surgery. That day, my oldest son was due to write his high school admission test. I obviously couldn't go because I was in the hospital, so my friend took him to take the test. They came back as I was leaving for surgery.

Somehow, when I was still on the stretcher and at the door of the operating room, I saw him and my friend and just smiled at them. I asked if he had passed his test. He nodded in confirmation that yes, he had passed. I smiled. When the stretcher went in, I was so happy, and I had this big smile on my face.

My eyes were glowing, and the doctors in the room noticed and told me, "You look so excited to be having heart surgery." Everyone else started smiling. I said, "I have to say something." They said, "Yes, please speak up. Do you want to meet anyone?" Because it's a big surgery. I said, "No. I just wanted to say, even if I die today, I will be the luckiest and the most successful person."

The doctors' reaction was unexpected. They were confused at my excitement. Of course, they didn't have any background or context about what I was saying. So, they smiled and said, "No, no, you should be fine."

I said, "No, because my son got admitted to high school and I'm very happy about it. Even if I'm dead, I know my kids will go to school." To this day, I still remember the expressions on their faces.

It wasn't like my son got admitted to Harvard. I was so excited about him getting into high school. They didn't realize that was such a significant thing for me. My kids had missed so much school during the divorce, when we were in Dubai and then to come to a new country, with a new language and do so well, ensured me that no matter what happened, they would succeed.

After that, I remember one of the doctors came in and patted my shoulder. He asked if we were good to go, and I said yes. When they give you anesthesia, they ask you to count backward. I remember that I started counting, and then I was gone. The last memory I had was my son finally going to school. Obviously, I came through the surgery and it was successful.

How to Find Your Inner Calling

After I got home from the surgery, I started thinking, "What if I had died that day? What if I hadn't survived the surgery or the post-surgery?" I would have left this world without thanking the people who had been there for me and the boys. I would have left the world without creating a legacy for my kids to follow. I would have left the world without completing the things that God wanted me to deliver, or without fulfilling my purpose in this world.

I was confused, sad and concerned all at the same time. How could I give back to the community, to the people who had done so much for me?

For some, it is the crisis in life that allows you to find your inner calling. I was now a heart surgery survivor. There will be limitations and restrictions for me to live a normal life, and I felt like there was no time to waste. Everything had brought me up to this time in my life.

It wasn't easy. There were nights I would cry and question myself. Why was I going through all of this? What have I done? Those were the questions I had for God. I went between fighting with him and questioning why this was happening to me, as all humans do.

All I knew was that God wanted me to do something bigger than life, and I needed to put everything in place.

I could hear the inner calling. I was not clear what that inner calling was, but I knew there was a purpose that God wanted me to deliver. Whatever I had gone through and survived, it was not to just go to work and raise kids and that was it. There was something else, and I was struggling to figure out what it was.

It was during that time that I started talking to my friend, the one I call my soulmate. I told him that I felt like I have a purpose in life, but I did not know what it was, and that I felt so lost. I felt that I was being selfish not doing it or feeling incompetent not being able to decode the inner calling that was coming to me. I did not know what to do.

He said, "Why don't you start doing some volunteer work and see where it leads to? Maybe you will know exactly what it is you want to do." I told him I was new in Connecticut and I did not know where to go and he gave me a direction. He suggested that I go to the refugee services here in Connecticut, and then maybe the Chamber of Commerce because I had so much experience in marketing and branding. I had a good business background that I had developed from the years working at my job. He said, "Go and talk to them and maybe you will find something there."

After he left, I was thinking, "How could the Chamber of Commerce be the answer to my calling? What am I supposed to do there?"

I was lost. I could hear my purpose calling deep inside of me, but I could not decode it. So, I decided to try both places. That's when I went to the refugee center and asked how they wanted me to help.

Taking The Plunge Towards a Purpose

They were very excited, even before knowing my story. I didn't tell them my story. I just walked in as a volunteer, and they were excited.

[132]

After a week or so, I shared my story with them. They said, "Oh my gosh, you can do so many things." So, I said, "Okay, let us start with what I can do right now."

We realized that the refugee families who come from war zone areas like Iraq, Iran, and Syria, are brought to the U.S. and they don't speak English. In those countries, they are brought up where the men take initiative and learn the skills because they are the ones who work and earn money for the family. When those refugee families come in, it's only the men who focus on getting acclimated to the culture and learning the language or skills to get a job. Not the women.

I sat with this refugee center and said, "What is holding the women back from stepping up and doing something to help support their families?" The biggest problem was language – speaking English. We needed people to teach them English.

We started a program called Mommy and Me, where the mothers and their children were called into a classroom environment and we started teaching them English. They learned day to day English, just enough to help them become capable of expressing themselves. They could go to the market and buy things, and if there was an issue with their kids, they could go to the hospital and talk to the doctor or communicate with 911 if they had to call an ambulance. Just the simple basics.

The plan was to help them learn English skills. When they are able to communicate, they will feel like they are part of the culture, part of the society, and they will make connections. Then they would want to grow more and learn more skills. That would be the next step.

First, we let them go through this phase, and then we would start teaching them skills. If they already had some skills, we would help them to master them and share the gifts they already have with the world. Some of them were really good at handicrafts, embroidery, painting, cooking, and those types of skills. This would all come later. The first step was helping them feel like part of the community.

For the children, we would also help prepare them. We had more volunteers coming in and would prepare the children to go to school. They would otherwise just end up in school without knowing the language.

This was the program I started volunteering for, and it was so rewarding. Whenever I would go to the program and come back home, I had this feeling that maybe these women needed me. Maybe these kids needed me. My group and I were working so closely, and I was helping others.

I was so thankful. My kids and I did not have the language barrier. We were born to a privileged family. We had been able to go to school and get an education. For us, our challenges were different.

For people who do not have the basic language in their hands, things are more difficult. At least I was helping them to take another step. Somehow, I felt that peace and comfort deep inside of me. I thought, "Okay, maybe this is the calling."

It wasn't the full yes, but I could feel my discomfort transforming into a little comfort zone. When I started going to the Chamber, it was more about, "What do I do now?" I still was not allowed to work, so my focus was solely on making a difference.

Find Your Purpose And The Rest Will Fall Into Place

This is such an important lesson to learn, and I really want to emphasize this.

Find your purpose. Find your passion and try to decode the inner calling rather than focusing on the reward you will get. The reward part comes later. If you are aligned with your purpose, and you start to act on it, things will come together.

When I went to the Chamber of Commerce, I told them I wanted to volunteer. I submitted my resume and told them to let me know what I could do for them.

They said they have women entrepreneurs coming in looking for someone to guide them through the process and show them how to write a business plan, explain what branding is, show them how to do their logo, show them how to do pricing and market analysis, and all of that. They needed someone to guide them.

Money Shouldn't be The Reason – It Should be the Outcome

During all of the work that I was doing with the Chamber of Commerce, I found the Cherry Blaire Foundation in the U.K. They are business mentors who work with women in third world countries to help them start their entrepreneurial journey. They needed mentors to work with the women to guide them through the process.

It is a strict selection process. I applied with them and told them I was already volunteering in these areas with the Chamber of Commerce, West Haven. I was selected. I am still a mentor for Cherry Blaire Foundation. It is so much fun and rewarding.

As I volunteered for the Chamber, word started to spread about me and my skills. People started reaching out to me and referring me to others. There came a point when my friend told me, "It looks like you're really happy in doing what you're doing. Helping women and also men start to transform their lives."

It was a turning point in my life. My purpose was clear. I was to transform lives by helping people understand who they are, accept it, then believe in themselves and shine.

When I talk to people and help businesses, the first thing I start with is, "Let's talk about your purpose."

It is the passion that you deliver during your work that makes you an expert. When I am working with my clients, I know I am working on their dreams. Making money is part of it, but money is like a form of energy. It is the same thing as eating. When you consume food, you get the energy to run, to talk, to learn, and more.

So, similarly, when you work on your passion, you release passion in the form of money, in the form of fame, or recognition. From that money, you do things for the world. You may discover something, invent something, or become part of running a business and delivering something great.

Money is an energy or an outcome. It should never be the reason. It should be the outcome of whatever you do for your purpose.

When you are looking for your purpose, slow down and explore. I promise you it is worth it. As you know from previous chapters, that time of exploration and volunteering led me to start my own company, Nyn's Dreams. I help entrepreneurs live their dream by helping them with their purpose, business plans, and marketing. Now I get to live my dream to make other people's dreams come true.

Your purpose is waiting for you to find it. Your job now is to start the search and trust that it will find you when you are ready.

Chapter 13:

Making Your Dreams a Reality

*The future belongs to those who believe
in the beauty of their dreams.*

Eleanor Roosevelt

When I started Nyn's Dreams, I was still working full-time. I don't like when people say to give up your 9-to-5 job, or that your 9-to-5 job makes you a slave. I stop them right there. The experts say that you can either be an entrepreneur or an employee. That is not true, you can be both. There may come a time when your business grows so big that you need to make a choice, but that is different. We see on social media, coaches and everyone else promoting the entrepreneurial journey against your employment, or against you as an employee. I want to encourage people to dive a little deeper before declaring entrepreneurship as the only way of living a happy and fulfilled life.

I have always loved my full-time job. As you can see, that job has helped me throughout my journey and my struggles. It kept me alive as I learned new things, explored different opportunities, experienced life, and started finding my purpose. I realized that as much as I enjoy my job and it supports me financially, it was not in alignment with my purpose. That is when I started experimenting with ideas to build my business around my purpose.

It's All About Finding a Balance

I am passionate about what I do, and I enjoy it. I never feel like my job or my business is a burden. Of course, with age, energy levels drop and there is only so much you can do in a day. There are times that I feel overwhelmed having to both work at my job and run my business.

But that's the choice I make. The business keeps me very close to my purpose. I only take the work I can do. I know that I cannot expand at the moment because I'm committed to something else. That commitment is bringing in a stable income, which I need at this point. If you think that you can continue and survive and do your business, fair enough. If you can't, do not feel guilty about it.

I also include volunteer time in my business. The first two or three sessions that I do with my clients are complimentary, until I find that they have a purpose, or I have helped them to find a purpose in their business. I charge a fee when we do the transactional work. The first three sessions are complimentary because it's more about discovering yourself. Discovering one's own-self is my passion, and I do not mix my passion with money.

That is the thing I want to do. I want to spend as much of my time with the client to understand what they want and how they want to grow within their business. Once we're ready and aligned on that, then the transactional part comes in. That would be the business plan, branding, and everything else for the business. This is when I start charging them.

My exact purpose is to help people live their dreams, live the life they want, and live the dream they see for themselves. I'm committed to guiding people to embrace their own reality with expansive thoughts and actions for a successful life and career.

Own Your Story and Start Living Your Dream

The biggest thing that holds us back from winning big or not been able to live the life we would love to live, is our strong belief in our limiting thoughts. We start looking at life from the perspective of lack and thus end up living a life full of disappointment, anger, hatred, frustration, and judgement.

Even before we know it, this energy of lack, self-doubt, and fear seeps into every area of our lives and we see devastating results in both our personal and professional lives.

When we decide to shift from the space of lack towards pure potentiality, we start believing in ourselves and step up to make our dreams come true. We shift gears from playing victim to champion. When we believe in ourselves and own our story, we are ready to navigate the wide spectrum of abundance. We take risks, we become fearless, we aim for winning, we learn, we focus on our goals, and in the process, we not only find our purpose but also spread our wings to help others to live a better life.

Over the years, I've seen my family members, friends and colleagues reaching out to me to share their wins, challenges, and even failures. I

[142]

have always been their go-to person to gain clarity or focus in life. It feels good to be there for others. I intentionally practice kindness, compassion, and empathy because it all comes naturally to me.

Soon these values started emerging as my personal brand because the world could see it all the way through my thoughts, words, and deeds. It was only because I was able to identify my passion that I could build an authentic personal brand.

The world started noticing and it helped immensely in my career. I'm paid for all my technical expertise but valued and appreciated for who I am. My colleagues and senior leadership would stretch me into projects and events that demanded more human connection. Now, I get the honor of working in the Diversity and Inclusion Council for the North American region. Now, my passion is seen. Everyone knows it, and I own my story – however painful it is. I was ashamed of it at one point. Now, I'm not, because I am who I am because of it.

When you own your story, you start sharing your truth with the world, and you make your personal brand visible.

It's very important for a human being to own their story. Accept yourself, and then go into the world and share your gifts.

I challenge my clients to look beyond their limiting beliefs, I help them navigate their strengths and reset their inner compass towards the direction of their dreams. I encourage them to emerge as purpose-driven leaders and operate from their zone of genius.

Don't Hide Behind a False Appearance

At the onset of my entrepreneurial journey with different chambers, I started working more on referrals. I don't spend a lot of money on marketing, yet I invest a lot of time and energy into networking. Human connection is still a winner even in this digital era. Everything I get is from my referrals.

It is researched and known now that just 20% of opinions and buying decisions are based on what you know, and a big 80% are based on who you are, whether you're conscious of it or not.

Personal Brand is not just being who you are, but to amplify and accentuate the best of who you are just like the people you admire… just like the Browns, the Oprah's and the Robin Sharma's. So finding your own personal brand is all about identifying that spark inside of yourself and letting it shine, so you can impact the lives of thousands of people just by being more of who you are.

Let me share an example with you; Oprah Winfrey. She doesn't have the fittest figure but she loves herself for who she is. Many people define her personal brand to be her perfectly done hair, chic yet modest professional clothing and shiny heels. But her wide, infectious smiles radiate her inner confidence. Oprah has branded herself as the woman people turn for help and advice. She has weaved her core values involving love, acceptance, self-realization, and humility so profoundly that her work and her business brand all speak through her and have amplified her success.

Similarly, if you go to a Nike store or a Levi's store, you know what is happening there every single day. Their commitment to sustainability, diversity, and inclusion, and not giving up on your dreams can be seen and felt everywhere.

Even if you are coming on social media every single day, share your authentic self to the world. It will do miracles for you and your business.

Remember, every single thing about how you present yourself online and offline is a signal you're sending to your prospect. Do not underestimate the power of your authentic personal brand and then weave it into your business. This will empower you to be in a position of control where you can take responsibility for how you're showing up in the world and getting noticed to create incredible impact and income.

Success Brings Contentment

The definition of success is going to be different for everyone. The bottom line is that the one element that is constant in every definition of success is contentment. When you are doing everything in alignment with your purpose, contentment will come. When there is contentment, there is truth.

At the moment, I'm happy with all the clients I have, because I'm content in what I'm doing. I'm trying to build it bit by bit, and grow step by step so that I don't lose that contentment. I am putting all of the right bricks together. I'm stacking them in the right direction and cementing them with a purpose every time, so that the foundation remains strong.

I encourage people to stay true to their core values while making tough business/executive decisions. I want you to know yourself, be yourself and put yourself out in the world authentically, unapologetically & powerfully. You will create an influential personal brand to scale-up your business, become an authentic leader and have fulfilling relationships.

If you are interested in finding out more about how I can help you find your entrepreneurial purpose and create an influential personal brand to scale-up your business, become an authentic leader and have fulfilling relationships, go to https://www.nynsdreams.com/newhome01/cons ulting-services/ and book a time to talk. Your business will grow when you are in congruence with your identity, purpose, and action.

What happens within you determines what is possible in your life.

Chapter 14:

Learning The Art of Forgiveness

Forgiveness is the attribute of the strong.

Mahatma Gandhi

H ow do you deal with people who don't like you or even hate you?

I had a client a few months ago that came to me because she was starting a jewelry business. She said she wanted to hire me to help launch her business, meaning helping her with branding and pricing and those details. We started talking about it. After a couple days, she called me and said, "You know, I just love you, and I love your work and everything, but I am scared."

[149]

I asked her why she was scared, and she said she was afraid to give me the liberty and space to launch her business because I didn't have experience in selling jewelry. She said, "There's nothing in your portfolio that indicates that you helped a jewelry business."

I looked at her and said, "It's not about products." If you have skills in marketing, branding, and product positioning, you can sell anything. You can sell a refrigerator or jewelry.

But she said, "No, because you don't know." She said she was sure. She told me, "You do so much work in apparel, footwear, salons, and cafes, but you haven't done jewelry and I'm not comfortable. How would you know about the topaz or sapphire or anything else? And the photography – how would you know what angle to take or not to take, or how to guide the photographer? My branding could be impacted."

She just went into that negative mode, and the words and language that she was using started to degrade me, implying that I didn't deserve it. We hadn't signed a contract at that time.

As a human, I felt offended. What is she trying to say? Is she saying I don't know branding? I could feel that negative discomfort crawling up my spine every time she spoke.

I asked her if we could meet again in the next few days, and she said yes. I told her to think it over, and I would do the same. When we met again, I told her I was not doing the project and she was free to connect with someone she felt was better to brand her. She said she would do that, and that she thought it was the best thing to do.

Usually when I am talking to a new client and having discovery calls, I talk to my friends and team members and let them know what we're getting with that new client. I'll tell them we are expecting this new client and what the value could be, and other details.

When I told them that this particular client was over, everyone said, "It's your ego. You should have convinced her. You should have shown her the work you do. You stopped because she said things that you didn't like about your work and capabilities. Your ego was hurt and you just said no to her. That's not the best way to do business."

I asked them to pause there for a while. I explained that it was in the best interest of both parties. That lady was already in doubt about my work. If she hadn't have told me, things would be different, but she did tell me that she's not confident in me.

So now, whatever I do, even if I design her a logo or propose her a pricing strategy, she will come back and comment both the positive and negative. If she comments negatively, I would be judgemental and would not have taken it as a genuine comment. I would have said that she has fears and doubts because she doesn't like working with me. Even if I did an incredible job but she doesn't like it, I will think that no matter what I do, she won't like it.

So, if that happened, I wouldn't attempt to improve my work. I would judge her reviews and feedback, and it could get really messy. The same goes for her. Even if I do my best work, she would still be hesitant to accept it and integrate it into the business because she would be wondering if it will work or not.

I told my team and my friends that it was in the best interest of both the parties to give this up. They found it to be a sentimental approach, not a logical one, and they didn't like it.

So, the contract went away. After a few months, she called me and said, "You know what, Nageen, I want to have a contract with you and you're the only person who can do this for me." I

[152]

asked if she was still selling jewelry, and she said yes. She wanted to go global and believed that there was no one else who could help her with global branding and marketing other than me.

I said okay, and we signed the contract. Now, things were different. Now, she had this confirmation that I could do it. I also know that she does like me. When I deliver something, even if she doesn't like it a million times, I keep trying and giving her new things with the same passion. I try to make things work because I know that she isn't judgemental. It's coming from a clean heart and a clean mind. There is no prejudice there.

Eliminate Hatred From Your Attitude

The reason I mention this incident is because it's the same way you deal with the people who hate or don't like you. There was no hate in this example, but there was dislike or doubt. That leads to hatred.

Hatred is a strong word. I usually ask people to avoid it. People use that word so often. For example, they'll say, "I hate the color blue," or, "I hate heels on me," or, "I hate guys wearing black." We use this word a lot. Wouldn't it be better if you said dislike instead of hate? That is a more accurate word.

[153]

Even for people, we say, "Oh, I hate that person." Why would you hate that person? Hate leads to revenge. It leads to negative circumstances. You could end up killing someone because you hate them. Why would you do that? Why would you hate anybody?

I do not like the word hate. I always tell people to dilute it. There are other ways of saying you don't like something or that you don't connect with something instead of saying you hate it. There are people in the world you don't like. There are people who also don't like you, and that's okay. That is perfectly fine, and it's normal.

It's even true within your family. If you have four or five siblings, you may have a stronger connection to one of them than the other three or four. Among your parents, you may be more connected to your mom than your dad. This variation in the degree of how strong your connection is with them is not the definition of hate. It's the ability to connect and accept the other person. The person you love has a few things in them that you may not like, but if that is part of the person you love, you will ignore it.

For example, my younger brother has an attitude toward life where he doesn't care about people.

We lost our dad at a young age and he grew up as a boy without a father, so he has a different mindset and approach to things. For him, his thinking is, "I don't give a damn about the world because the world has nothing to do with who I am today." In my opinion, he has a bad attitude.

If someone invited my brother to a party and he can't go, he will say, "No, I don't want to come." That person would feel offended. If I am invited to a party and am unable to go, it would take me about five minutes to say no. That person has taken the time to invite me to their joys and celebrations, and because I don't want to be there, or I don't want that company, I just tell them I'm happy for them. I'll say that I wish I could make it but that I already have a commitment to attend, but that I wish them all the best or ask if they need help. My brother finds that all BS, in his words. He thinks if you don't want to go, don't go, and that you don't have to care about the world.

I love my brother, but I don't like his careless attitude. I don't become friends with people who have this attitude, but because this is my brother whom I love, I ignore it or try to counsel him about it.

[155]

Hatred itself is so powerful. I tell people that every word you say, every email you write, every interaction with people, creates your image and builds your empire or credibility. If you use the word hate so often, even in small things, it brings negative energy. Then you start living with that negative energy.

First of all, get rid of this hate thing. Now, let's talk about forgiveness.

Forgiving Isn't Forgetting

Here is an honest confession. This is the most important one I will make in this book. There is a difference between forgiving and moving on.

It's not important to forgive to move on. That's what I feel. People preach that forgiveness is divine, and it is, so it needs a lot of energy. Because it is divine, it's not easy for humans to do.

If you are struggling, the best thing is to forgive. but honestly, if you cannot forgive, just don't hold onto it. Move on and think that whatever that person has done, it's because it's the only thing they could have done. If he could have done anything other than what he had done, he would have done it. It was beyond his capability and capacity as a human being. Just leave things there, take your own path, and move on.

[156]

If you ask me today honestly, I cannot forgive the man that was so brutal to me. He physically, emotionally, and financially abused me. He was never there as a father for my kids. Whatever grudges he had against me is one thing, but the children are his children. He has never looked for them, never worried about them, thought about them, or contacted them. As a human being, I am weak. I honestly can't forgive him.

At the same time, I'm strong enough to leave things there and move on with good things. I move on with the things that I want to do in life, and not just talk about it every time in a negative way and convey that to my kids as well.

After the divorce, there were very few instances where my kids and I sat together and talked about the bad times we had because of that man. I avoid that. I do not do that.

At the end of the day, he is their father. I wanted them to make the decision to connect with him at some point or not. That is the independent decision that they have to make. They cannot be disrespectful to him at any time, because of something their mother taught them. They have to respect him as their father. Whether they choose to meet him or connect with him is their choice. They don't have to be disrespectful about it or abuse him.

God forbid, if they do anything, or develop anger-management issues and then say, "Oh, it's because we inherited it from our father," or, "We had a difficult childhood and that's why it's in us." You cannot have an excuse to be wrong.

Deep down inside my heart, I wish that someday I could become so powerful that I could say I've forgiven everyone who has hurt me. Right now, at this moment, I am not that strong. I am weak enough not to forgive, but I'm strong enough to leave things as they are and then move on.

For example, if you get a bruise on your hand or feet, and then it becomes so messy that it spreads and ends up leaving a scar on your skin, what do you do? Do you talk about it daily, even if people aren't looking at it? Do you say, "See, I have this scar because of something, and it was so painful?" No, you don't. The scar is there but your hand is working. You are functioning as a normal human being with that foot that has the scar, or your hand that has the scar, or the face that has a scar.

But that doesn't mean that the scar isn't there. It doesn't mean that the pain wasn't there. It's there, but it becomes insignificant.

The Art of Learning Forgiveness

You don't have to forgive everyone, but you don't have to talk about it every time. If you do, you are living the same way as the person who hates you.

My advice to everyone is to try and forgive. That's the best thing to do. If someone can do that, I salute them. That is so powerful. But if not, don't use it as an excuse every time to tell people about any of their shortcomings or your negative actions. That's not what that is. You don't have to hold revenge in your heart. That's important.

Forgiveness is one thing, but then you don't have to have revenge in your heart. You don't have to say something like, "This guy deserves this." How do you know that? I don't like it when people say someone deserved that. Really? How do you know they deserved that? Just because someone did one bad thing to you doesn't mean that they deserve a bad life.

Get out of that self-God complex.

How would you feel if something bad happens to you and someone says you deserve it, do you really?

The only thing we deserve as human beings is goodness from each other. Other than that, what happens is just the reactions to the actions – our approach and attitude towards life. This is very important.

Trust and Proper Boundaries

When we talk about trust, we can go back to that client I mentioned. She initially dumped me, and then came back to me with trust. You can see that I still remember her and what she said to me. But then, I had this positive side and made the right decision. This was something that was important, and when she came back, I wasn't judgemental. I said, "Okay. Let's do it together." And we did.

Forgiveness doesn't mean trust. These are two completely different elements. I don't know why people always try to bring them together and marry them.

Today, if my ex-husband were to come to me and sincerely ask for forgiveness, and I forgave him, does that mean I have to trust him? I have seen him fail me so many times that I will never be able to have that trust.

If there is trust, if there is truth, all of the other things will fall into place. Trust me. This is how it works.

[160]

Nyn Riffat

If you are truthful to yourself and you're
speaking truth every day, you're building
credibility and gaining another person's trust.
People start trusting you because you have
always spoken the truth.

Forgiveness does not create trust, but if you're
truthful and you've built the bond of trust, it
won't guarantee forgiveness, but it will increase
the chances of receiving it.

If you continue to share your truest self to your
friends, your family members, or your partners,
they become used to seeing you as a true person.
They start trusting you and you start trusting
them. When they do something wrong and they
come out and realize they've done something
wrong and come to you again, you don't judge
them. By that time, all of your consistent
behavior of being truthful will have created a
strong bond of trust.

There are many shades on every journey;
connecting to the past and knowing the truth
makes us both bruised and beautiful.
I have been through hell and back but I'm
grateful for every scar. The trajectory of life gives
you the experience of betrayals and heartbreaks
in many forms; you will have disappointments
in partnerships both at professional and personal

[161]

levels; you will experience your loved ones questioning your worth; you will be doubted and challenged and these all will leave you feeling neglected, lost and vulnerable. Through it all you will learn to cry, laugh and grow.

I look at myself in my 20's and see a young soul believing in the beauty of her dreams; unaware of the cruel and brutal shades of this thing called LIFE. I now see a woman who is striving to help many to transform their dreams into reality. I'm in a phase of gratitude right now.

With truth as your superpower, I encourage you to keep improving, evolving, moving forward, inspiring, teaching and learning till your last breath.

Leave the Bad and Take the Good

When people ask me if I have forgiven my ex-husband, I only smile. I don't give details. It is not something I need to share with everyone. My kids know the truth and that is what is important. To be a good mother while my heart was breaking, and to stick to the values of my dad while my existence was bleeding are two of the hardest roles I've ever had to play.

I would suggest this to everyone. If you are going into a difficult phase, whether it's with your business, your past, your brothers and

[162]

sisters, or if it's just a critical phase, leave it and move on. Take the best from it and move on. Your life is not between the moments of your birth and death. Your life is between now and your next breath. The present, the here and now is all the life you ever get.

When people talk about how bad their previous job was, for example in interviews, they don't have to do a character assassination for that boss. There's no reason to sit in front of a new hiring manager and say negative things about a past manager. It's unnecessary.

There are difficult situations, but park them and move on. From difficult situations, you learn many things. Maybe you learned when to be quiet and calm, or maybe you learned new skills.

There are moments when I wish I could roll back the clock and take all the sadness away. But I also know that if I somehow could roll it back, all the joy I've experienced would be gone as well. And the reality is, I can't change the past anyway. No one can. The past must be accepted. When you accept the past, regardless of how painful, you allow yourself to grow and heal. For example, if someone breaks your heart, it's not easy to deal with, but you can heal, as long as you're willing to accept the circumstances and

[163]

then gradually let them go. That's reality. Accepting that reality, and everything that follows, is part of letting go and growing from it. You don't get to choose what is true. You only get to choose how you respond to it.

With my ex-husband, I don't remember a lot of good things. But whenever I share my story, my focus is more around the lessons that I have learned from those painful experiences and not about the character or behaviour of my ex-husband.

I want you to be free from hate, whether it be inside of you or thrown at you from the outside. Hate leaves you empty and unhappy. Learn to let it go. Forgive when you can and then let it go, so you can live your best life possible.

Chapter 15:

It's Your Turn

*Find the strength to leave in the past
those parts of your life that are over, so
you can better attend to the present.*

What a journey this has been, and I can`t believe that this part is almost complete. My goal is to help you to see that no matter what you go through in life, you can overcome it and have a successful life. The only reason your past can stop you is if you let it.

Having a marriage dissolved and the struggle for the custody of my sons was beyond painful for me, but out of ashes, something was birthing. I had an unarguable desire to make an impact, to lead, to claim my voice, and so I started this book.

Writing this book has also been part of my healing and becoming stronger. As I shared with you what I went through, it allowed me to let it go even more. Now it is out of me and treasured on these pages where it can help you, so thank you for reading this book and allowing me to open up my heart to you. Remember that you will always grow from your space of strength.

My Biggest Takeaways

As I go back through this book, I want to share some final thoughts on what I have learned. These are my biggest aha's that have changed my life and allowed me to transform my life.

Believe In Yourself

This one is crucial. You will never move forward unless you believe you can. Here is the wonderful thing about belief. It takes very little to accomplish great things. Think of it as seed. The potential for the biggest trees we know, started with something that fits on your fingertip or in the palm of your hand.

Size does not matter. It is what you do with it that counts. If you are willing to take that first step, you will be amazed at what happens when it starts to grow.

Maybe you don`t have any belief right now. That is ok, borrow some of mine. I know that you can do this. You were created with a uniqueness that equips you to not only survive what has happened but thrive past it. I believe in you.

My friend Sherine always felt like the invisible girl. Everyone would think of her when they needed a favour or help, but otherwise, they did not think about her at all. This left Sherine believing that she wasn't important, and she didn't have any contributions to make to the world, so she didn't try.

As an adult, she realized that she never allowed her uniqueness to shine. She stayed in the background because that is where she believed she belonged. Now it was time for her to come into the light. It was hard, and fear fought her for a long time, but as she took those first steps, she knew that this was what she was created for; to shine and serve others.

Now Sherine loves what she does, is good at it, and others recognize it too. Now people come to her, and she gets to help them in amazing ways. Her belief is strong, which leads us to my next biggest aha…

Fear's Only Job Is To Destroy

Fear will never be your friend. It is always your enemy. It tricks you into thinking that it is there to help you when all it wants to do is destroy your destiny. Fear will give you all the excuses you need not to do the things you are supposed to do. Fear can come from within, but it can also be put upon you from the outside world. Whichever way it comes, there is only one thing you can do: don't accept it and always move forward.

It will fight you at first. You will feel it mentally, emotionally, and even physically. You have to choose to ignore it and do the things you are afraid to do. Once you do, you will see that it was merely a shadow, not a wall.

Fight For What Is Right

On your journey to becoming the person you were meant to be, you will have to fight for what is right. You will be given a choice between taking the more difficult choice, which is the right one, and the easier way out. The right way is always the best way, no matter how difficult it is. Taking the easier route only feels good for a short time, and then you start to pay the price of your choice. The opposite is true for the correct choice. It may be one of the hardest things you do, but the payoff for the rest of your life is worth it.

Everything that happens helps you grow, even if it's hard to see right now. Circumstances will direct you, correct you, and perfect you over time. Sometimes these circumstances knock you down, hard. There will be times when it seems like everything that could possibly go wrong is going wrong.

You might feel like you will be stuck in this rut forever, but you aren't. When you feel like quitting, remember that sometimes things have to go very wrong before they can be right. Sometimes you have to go through the worst, to arrive at your best because our most significant opportunities are often found in times of great difficulty.

I am forever grateful that I did not leave my boys and come to the U.S. by myself. They are the joy of my life, and I couldn't be prouder of the men that I know they will become. They are worth every sacrifice.

Integrity Counts

How you live your life is more important than what you do with it. When you are on your death bed, who is going to care? Will they be glad that you are going, or will people be weeping at your bedside wishing for one more day with you? You will miss out on opportunities that seem too good to be true, but when you live in integrity, it may move slower, but you will get there. Shortcuts will always come back to bite you later.

People Will Either Support You or Try to Destroy You

There will always be people who try to take the joy out of your life. They are jealous of the potential you have within you and will try to kill it before it has a chance to grow. You choose whether they will have that power in your life.

I stayed in an abusive relationship way longer than I should have. I allowed myself to be taken advantage of, and I took the restrictions placed on me to make someone else happy. Which it never did. It didn't matter what I did; my ex-husband was not going to love me or respect me. You will face your greatest opposition when you are closest to your biggest miracle.

To be loyal to yourself is to allow yourself to grow and change, and challenge who you once were and what you once thought. The only thing you ever have to be for sure is unsure, and this means you're growing, and not stagnant or shrinking.

Once I learned that it gave me the freedom to move forward and escape. I couldn't do it alone, and that is the other side of the coin. We cannot go through life without support from others. I am so thankful for those who came alongside me and helped me no matter what. They are true angels and deserve way more than I could ever pay back.

Never give in to the ones who hate you. Don't take their words into your heart. For those who love you, do everything you can to show them how much you care and extend all your support.

We all want to feel free from the stress of the world. Feel the fullness of who you are. You are important enough to care about yourself. Let today be the day when you free yourself from all the strings that were preventing you from doing good. It will cost you to release the old way of thinking, release the energetic attachment that is hurting and create an attachment with something more empowering.

Next Steps
What do you do now? I suggest you look back through the book again and underline the areas that catch your attention the most. Those are the

areas that you need to work on first. Those are the things where you need healing or training to move to the next step.

Then pick one and open up your heart to more. If you can, step up and forgive those who have hurt you, go ahead and do it. Let go of the past and work to embrace a new future. Recognize that it is a journey that will require time. Work towards growth. You don't manifest what you "want," you manifest what you "believe."

Then will come the day when you KNOW that you have to take action. Your next stage begins the moment that next step occurs. Don't be afraid, be bold and take that step knowing that the next one will be easier. Soon you will be running, and you will look back in amazement at how far you have come. You are made for greatness, and it is your time to shine.

I want to help you. I am at my happiest when I am helping others realize their big dreams. That is when I feel complete, whole and living my purpose.

Help me to live my dreams. I would love to talk to you about your journey and where you are at and the places you may need help. After so many successful years in corporate and then launching myself as a strong entrepreneur &

positivity influencer, I have a keen eye to spot simple things that may be holding you back from living the life of your dreams.

In closing, I would like to offer you a free consultation. Let's talk. Go to www.NynsDreams.com/contact, fill out the form, and I will email you back with my available times. In that call, I will help you to identify three problem areas and give you at least one solution that you can work on.

Thank you from the bottom of my heart for reading my book. I appreciate you more than you know, and it is my hope and prayer that this book has given you hope for the future.

As I go, I would like to leave you with my favourite quote. This one has become my mantra, and now I pass it on to you.

It doesn't matter who you are, where you come from. The ability to triumph begins with you - always.

Oprah Winfrey

Really, Truly

BElieve in **YOU**rself

Nyn Riffat

[173]

Made in the USA
Las Vegas, NV
03 May 2021